SUMMER BRAIN QUEST

Dear Parent,

At Brain Quest, we believe learning should be an adventure—a *quest* for knowledge. Our mission has always been to guide children on that quest, to keep them excited, motivated, and curious, and to give them the confidence they need to do well in school. Now, we're extending the quest to summer! Meet SUMMER BRAIN QUEST: It's a workbook. It's a game. It's an outdoor adventure. And it's going to stop summer slide!

Research shows that if kids take a break from learning all summer, they can lose up to three months' worth of knowledge from the previous grade. So we set out to create a one-of-a-kind workbook experience that delivers personalized learning for every kind of kid. Personalized learning is an educational method where exercises are tailored to each child's strengths, needs, and interests. Our goal was to empower kids to have a voice in what and how they learned during the summer, while ensuring they get enough practice with the fundamentals. The result: SUMMER BRAIN QUEST—a complete interactive program that is easy to use and designed to engage each unique kid all summer long.

So how does it work? Each SUMMER BRAIN QUEST WORKBOOK includes a pullout tri-fold map that functions as a game board, progress chart, and personalized learning system. Our map shows different routes that correspond to 110 pages of curriculum-based exercises and 8 outdoor learning experiences. The variety of routes enables kids to choose different topics and activities while guaranteeing practice in weaker skills. We've also included over 150 stickers to mark progress, incentivize challenging exercises, and celebrate accomplishments. As kids complete activities and earn stickers, they can put them wherever they like on the map, so each child's map is truly unique—just like your kid. To top it all off, we included a Summer Brainiac Award to mark your child's successful completion of his or her quest. SUMMER BRAIN QUEST guides kids so they feel supported, and it offers positive feedback and builds confidence by showing kids how far they've come and just how much they've learned.

Each SUMMER BRAIN QUEST WORKBOOK has been created in consultation with an award-winning teacher specializing in that grade. We cover the core competencies of reading, writing, and math, as well as the essentials of social studies and science. We ensure that our exercises are aligned to Common Core State Standards, Next Generation Science Standards, and state social studies standards.

Loved by kids and adored by teachers, Brain Quest is America's #1 educational bestseller and has been an important bridge to the classroom for millions of children. SUMMER BRAIN QUEST is an effective new tool for parents, homeschoolers, tutors, and teachers alike to stop summer slide. By providing fun, personalized, and meaningful educational materials, our mission is to help ALL kids keep their skills ALL summer long. Most of all, we want kids to know:

It's your summer. It's your workbook. It's your learning adventure.

—The editors of Brain Quest

This book belongs to:

Library of Congress Cataloging-in-Publication Data is available.

ISBN 978-0-7611-8917-6

Summer Series Concept by Nathalie Le Du, Daniel Nayeri, Tim Hall
Writers   Megan Hewes Butler, Claire Piddock
Consulting Editor   Mindy Yip
Art Director   Colleen AF Venable
Cover, Map, Sticker, and Additional Character Illustrator   Edison Yan
Illustrator   Rachel Dukes
Series Designer   Tim Hall
Designer   Abby Dening
Editor   Nathalie Le Du
Production Editor   Jessica Rozler
Production Manager   Julie Primavera

Workman books are available at special discounts when purchased in bulk for premiums and sales promotions as well as for fund-raising or educational use. Special editions or book excerpts can also be created to specification. For details, contact the Special Sales Director at the address below, or send an email to specialmarkets@workman.com.

DISCLAIMER
The publisher and authors disclaim responsibility for any loss, injury, or damages caused as a result of any of the instructions described in this book.

Workman Publishing Co., Inc.
225 Varick Street
New York, NY 10014-4381
workman.com

Printed in the United States of America
First printing March 2017

10 9 8 7 6 5

SUMMER BRAIN QUEST

BETWEEN GRADES 1&2

For adventurers ages 6–7

Written by Megan Hewes Butler and Claire Piddock
Consulting Editor: Mindy Yip

WORKMAN PUBLISHING
NEW YORK

4

Contents

Your Quest

Your quest is to sticker as many paths on the map as possible and reach the final destination by the end of summer to become an official Summer Brainiac.

Basic Components

Summer progress map

100+ pages of quest exercises

110 quest stickers

8 Outside Quests

8 Outside Quest stickers

Over 40 achievement stickers

Summer Brainiac Award

100% sticker

Setup

Detach the map and place it on a flat surface.

Begin at **START** on your map.

How to Play

To advance along a path, you must complete a quest exercise with the matching color and symbol. For example:

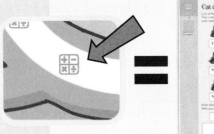

Math exercise from the orange level (Level 2)

English language arts exercise from the red level (Level 3)

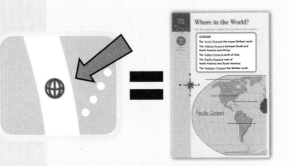

Social studies exercise from the blue level (Level 6)

Science exercise from the green level (Level 7)

If you complete the challenge, you earn a matching quest sticker.

Place the quest sticker on the path to continue on your journey.

At the end of each level, you earn an achievement sticker.

Apply it to the map and move on to the next level!

Outside Quests

Throughout the map, you will encounter paths that lead to Outside Quests.

To advance along those paths, you must complete one of the Outside Quests.

If you complete an Outside Quest, you earn an Outside Quest sticker and advance toward 100% completion!

Bonuses

If you complete a bonus question, you earn an achievement sticker.

BONUS: If the pig with the bow tie had to chop up 5 sticks instead of 3, how many sticks would be left?

_____ sticks left

→ Then add this sticker to your map!

Subject Completion

If you complete all of the quest exercises in a subject (math, English language arts, science, or social studies), you earn an achievement sticker.

CONGRATULATIONS!
You completed all of your science quests! You earned:

Summer Brainiac Award

Presented to:

for successfully completing the learning journey in
SUMMER BRAIN QUEST®: BETWEEN GRADES 1 & 2

Summer Brain Quest Completion Sticker and Award

If you complete your quest, you earn a Summer Brain Quest completion sticker and award!

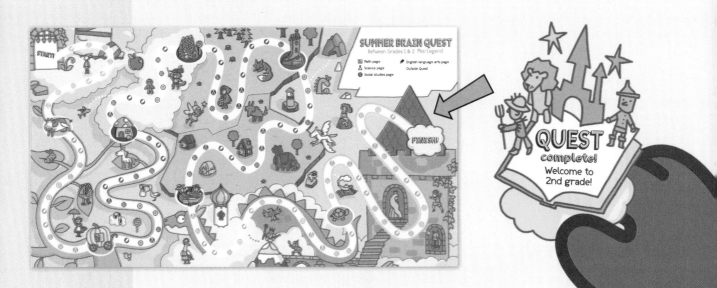

100% Sticker

Sticker *every* possible route and finish *all* the Outside Quests to earn the 100% sticker!

Level

1

Kickstart the Story!

Use a word from the box to make a compound word. Use each picture as a clue.

Compound Words

step	light	rain
	story	bean

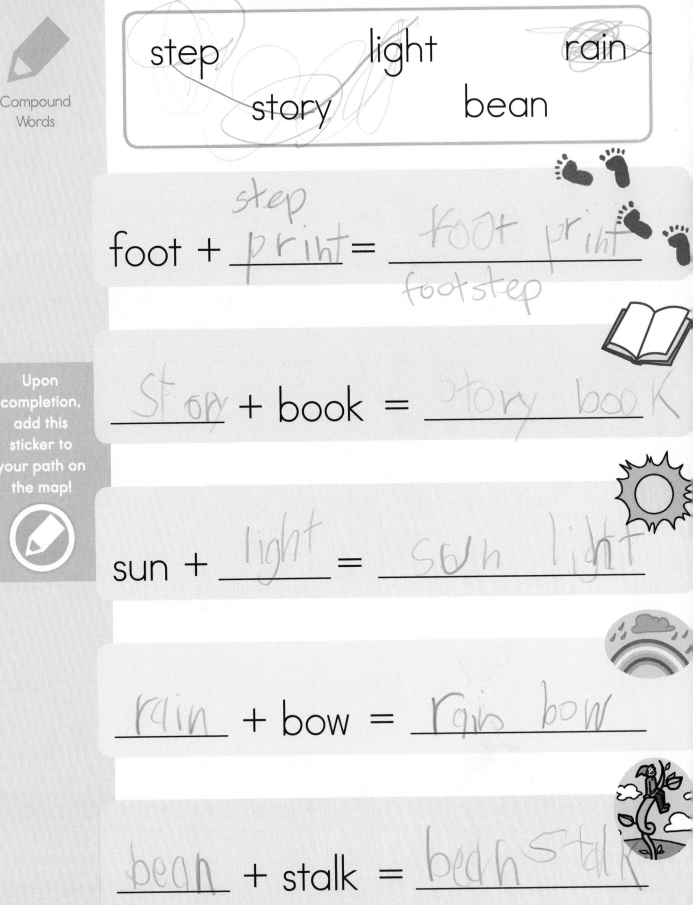

foot + ~~print~~ *step* = _footprint_
footstep

story + book = _story book_

sun + _light_ = _sun light_

rain + bow = _rain bow_

bean + stalk = _beanstalk_

Upon completion, add this sticker to your path on the map!

Where Jack Lives

Circle the objects Jack needs where he lives.

or

or

or

Draw a picture of the clothes or objects you need where you live.

Upon completion, add this sticker to your path on the map!

Brain Box

The **environment** that people live in affects their choice of where they live, what they wear, what type of food they eat, and how they travel.

Skip Counting

Even and Odd Leaves

Jack climbs only on the leaves with even numbers. Color the leaves with even numbers **green**. Color the leaves with odd numbers **orange**.

Upon completion, add this sticker to your path on the map!

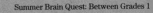

Jack's Beanstalk

Each part of this beanstalk plant has an important job.

Color the part that makes food **green**.

Color the part that collects water **blue**.

Color the part that carries water and nutrients yellow.

Color the part that makes seeds orange.

Upon completion, add this sticker to your path on the map!

BONUS: Circle the objects that Jack's beanstalk needs to grow.

Then add this sticker to your map!

Jack's Plan

Complete each word with a letter or letters from the box.

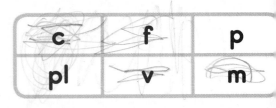

Word Family: -an

Upon completion, add this sticker to your path on the map!

_f_an

_P_lan

_M_an

_C_an

_v_an

_p_l_an

Jack has a plan. Make a prediction, and write or draw what he might do next!

Hey, Diddle, Diddle . . .

Write a sentence about the cat. What song might she be playing?

I made you
out of clay.

Write a sentence about the cow. Where could she be going?

The moon.

Addition

Apple-y Addition

Write the sum. Then draw lines to match the apples that have the same sum.

BONUS: Circle the apples that add up to 10. What other two numbers add up to 10? (HINT: There are a few possible pairs.)

Then add this sticker to your map!

$3 + 7 = 10$

$6 + 5 = 11$

$5 + 4 = 9$

$7 + 3 = 10$

$5 + 6 = 11$

$3 + 4 = 7$

$4 + 3 = 7$

$4 + 5 = 9$

Very Berry Addition

Addition

Draw a line to match each blackberry vine that has the same sum. (HINT: You can match the expressions without adding.)

3 + 5

7 + 4

2 + 12

5 + 3

5 + 8

8 + 5

4 + 7

12 + 2

Upon completion, add these stickers to your path on the map!

Wild Weather Report

Look at each picture and read the weather prediction. Then draw what might happen in such weather.

Weather

Upon completion, add this sticker to your path on the map!

weather prediction:
strong wind

weather prediction:
heavy rain

weather prediction:
hot temperatures

Level 1 complete!

Add this achievement sticker
to your path...

...and move on to

Level 2!

The Tortoise and the Hare

Read the story.

Once upon a time, there was a speedy hare who bragged, "I am the fastest animal of all!" A tortoise, tired of hearing the hare boast, challenged him, "Shall we race?" The hare laughed at the tortoise.

All of the animals came to watch the race. The race began and the hare sprinted ahead! The tortoise began walking at his slow and steady pace and didn't stop. The hare thought, "I am so fast! I have time to dance and relax!" He twirled and boogied. Then he sat down to rest and fell asleep.

The hare woke up when he heard cheering. "Hooray for the tortoise!" he heard. The hare walked to the crowd of animals at the finish line. "Slow and steady wins the race," said the tortoise to the hare.

Write or draw what lesson the tortoise learned.

Write or draw what lesson the hare learned.

Folktales

Upon completion, add these stickers to your path on the map!

Then add this sticker to your map!

BONUS: Which word describes the hare? Circle the best answer.

kind   unwise   smart

Cat and Fiddles

Look at the addition problem.
Then write the missing number in
each related subtraction problem.

| 3 | + | 6 | = | 9 |

| 9 | − | | = | 6 |

| 9 | − | | = | 3 |

What other two numbers can be subtracted to equal 6?
Write your own equation and draw a picture to illustrate it.

| | − | | = | 6 |

Cow and Moons

Draw the number of moons to show the addition problem. Then fill in the missing numbers for each related problem.

Addition and Subtraction

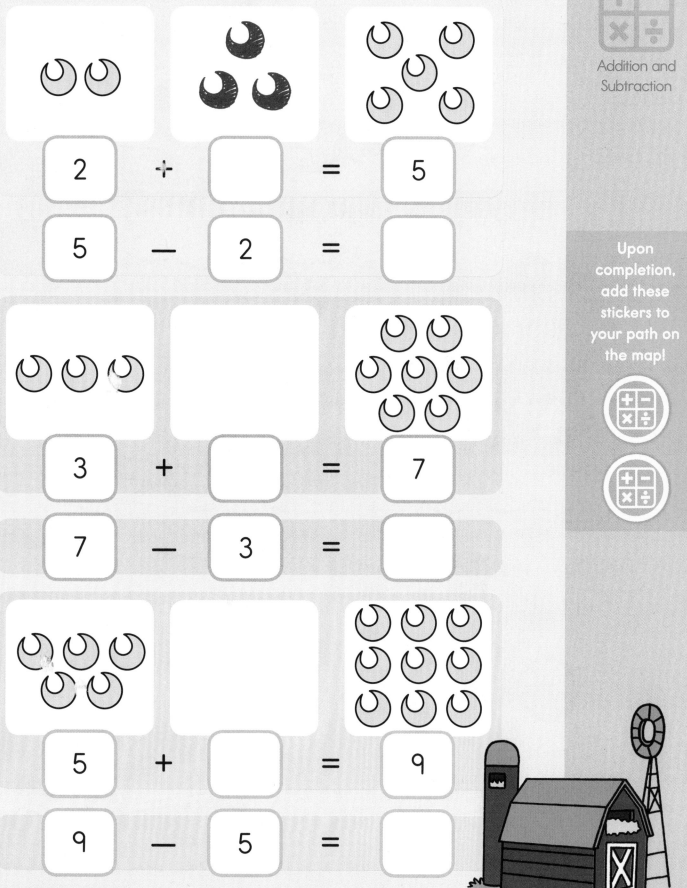

$2 + \boxed{} = 5$

$5 - 2 = \boxed{}$

$3 + \boxed{} = 7$

$7 - 3 = \boxed{}$

$5 + \boxed{} = 9$

$9 - 5 = \boxed{}$

Upon completion, add these stickers to your path on the map!

Transportation Throughout Time

People have traveled in different vehicles throughout time. Circle the pictures that show vehicles most frequently used in the past. Then underline the pictures of modern vehicles that we use today. (HINT: Some are the same vehicles that we used in the past!)

high-speed train

horse

sailboat

bike

car

jet

rowboat

buggy

biplane

Upon completion, add these stickers to your path on the map!

Make a prediction about how we will travel in the future.

Cinderella and the Glass Slipper

Draw each character to show her point of view.

CINDERELLA

Draw a picture of Cinderella cleaning the house.

Draw a picture of Cinderella getting ready for the Royal Ball.

WICKED STEPMOTHER

Draw a picture of the Wicked Stepmother giving Cinderella extra chores.

FAIRY GODMOTHER

Draw a picture of the Fairy Godmother helping Cinderella get to the ball.

Draw each setting to show where parts of the story take place.

CINDERELLA'S HOUSE

Draw a picture of the old house where Cinderella lived.

KING'S CASTLE

Draw a picture of the castle where Cinderella went to the ball.

Elements of a Story: Characters and Setting

Upon completion, add these stickers to your path on the map!

MOUSE HOLE

Cinderella made friends with the mice in her house. Draw a picture of what their home might have looked like.

Brain Box

Characters are the people or animals in a story. The **setting** is the location where a story takes place. There can be many characters and settings within the same story.

Forest Homes

Add or subtract. Write the answer.

$5 + 5 = \underline{}$

$8 + 1 = \underline{}$

$2 + 8 = \underline{}$

$3 + 6 = \underline{}$

3 + 3 = _____

$$\begin{array}{r} 10 \\ -5 \\ \hline \end{array}$$

$$\begin{array}{r} 2 \\ +6 \\ \hline \end{array}$$

$$\begin{array}{r} 9 \\ -1 \\ \hline \end{array}$$

7 − 4 = _____

BONUS: Baba Yaga takes 10 steps through the forest. You follow for 6 steps. Cross out the number of footsteps you have taken. Then write the difference.

10 − 6 = _____

Addition and Subtraction

Upon completion, add these stickers to your path on the map!

Then add this sticker to your map!

Plants All Over the World

Read about each plant. Then draw a line to match each plant to its habitat.

A **barrel cactus** stores water in its thick stem.

Pond

Some **orchids** grow in the shade of other plants.

Ocean

Moss grows close to the ground for protection from cold winds.

Desert

Kelp has deep roots to anchor it under rough water.

Rain Forest

Upon completion, add this sticker to your path on the map!

A **water lily**'s long stem holds its leaves above the water.

Arctic

Brain Box

A **habitat** is a natural home or environment for a plant or animal.

Different types of plants grow in different habitats.

Level 2 complete!

Add this achievement sticker
to your path...

...and move on to

Level

3!

Apple-y Words

Complete each word with a letter or letters from the box.

Word Family: -ap

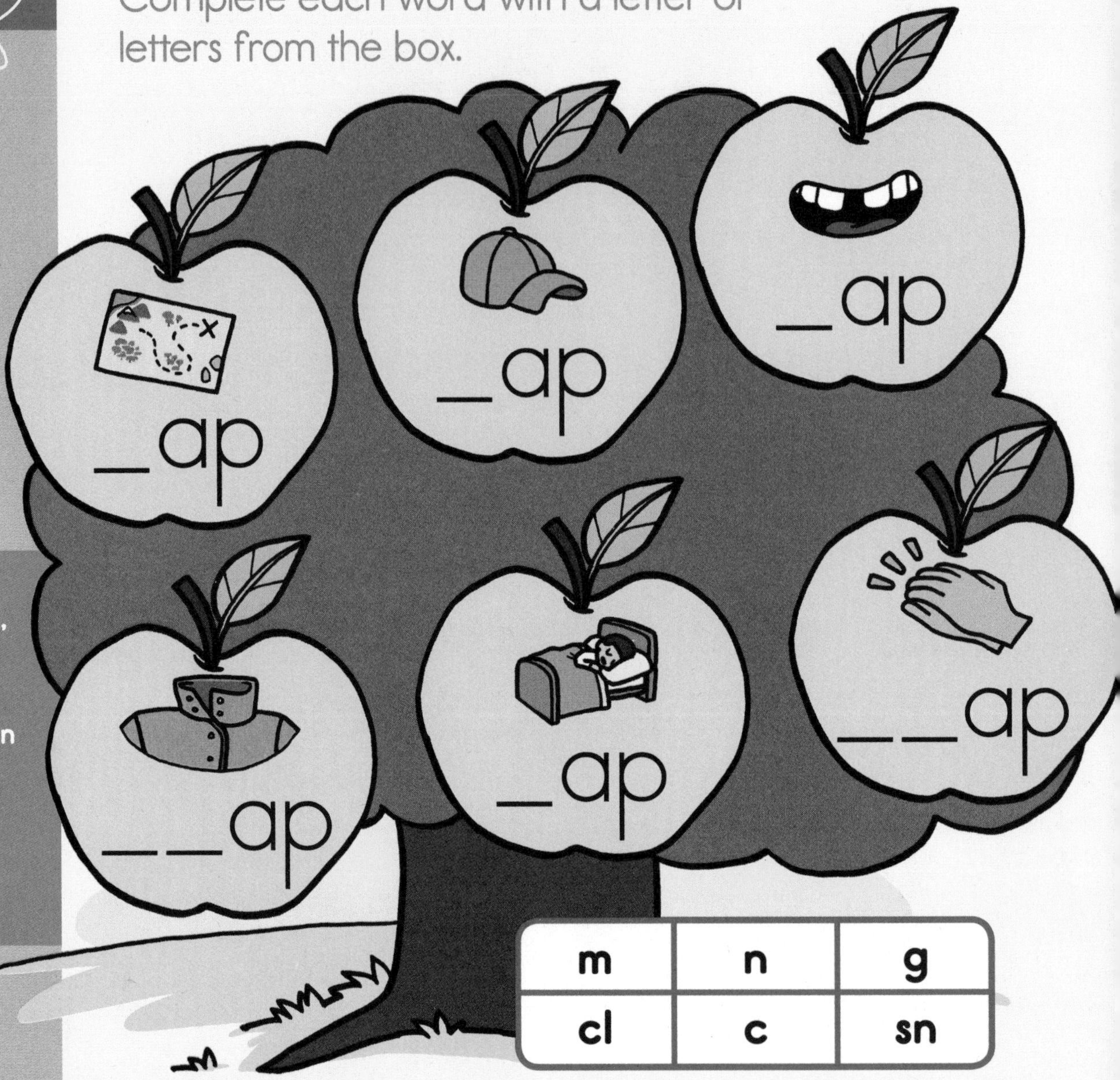

_ap

_ap

_ap

___ap

_ap

___ap

m	n	g
cl	c	sn

Upon completion, add this sticker to your path on the map!

BONUS: Complete this sentence:

The tired bird wants to ___ap.

Then add this sticker to your map!

The Golden Bird flaps his wings. Write or draw what he might fly toward.

In the Zone

On the map, draw buildings and places you might find in each zone. (HINT: Think about your own community. What kind of places are in each zone?)

Making a Map

Recreational

Commercial

Industrial

Residential

Upon completion, add this sticker to your path on the map!

BONUS: A candy factory is being built in your neighborhood— yum! Add it to your map in the correct zone.

Then add this sticker to your map!

Brain Box

Communities use land in different ways to meet people's needs.

An **industrial zone** is where goods are made.

A **commercial zone** is where people can buy goods and services.

A **recreational zone** is where people can play.

A **residential zone** is where people live.

Plant Survival

The Basic Needs of Plants

In each picture, a plant is not getting what it needs to grow. Draw what happens if the plant gets what it needs.

This fern has no water because of a drought.

→

Draw what will happen when it rains.

This plant has no light.

→

Draw what will happen when it's moved to a window.

TULIPS

These seeds have no soil for nutrients.

→

Draw what will happen when they are planted.

Brain Box

Plants get the energy they need from sunlight, and use air, water, and nutrients from the soil to make their food and grow.

Kitten Kin

Use the three numbers to complete the related math facts. They are a fact family!

Addition and Subtraction

Upon completion, add this sticker to your path on the map!

4 + 7 = ☐

7 + 4 = ☐

11 – 4 = ☐

11 – 7 = ☐

9 + 5 = ☐

5 + 9 = ☐

14 – 9 = ☐

14 – 5 = ☐

3 + 5 = ☐

5 + 3 = ☐

8 – 5 = ☐

8 – 3 = ☐

6 + 7 = ☐

7 + 6 = ☐

☐ – 6 = 7

☐ – 7 = 6

Reading a Map

Welcome to Candy Cloud

Follow the directions to read and complete the Candy Cloud map!

Upon completion, add these stickers to your path on the map!

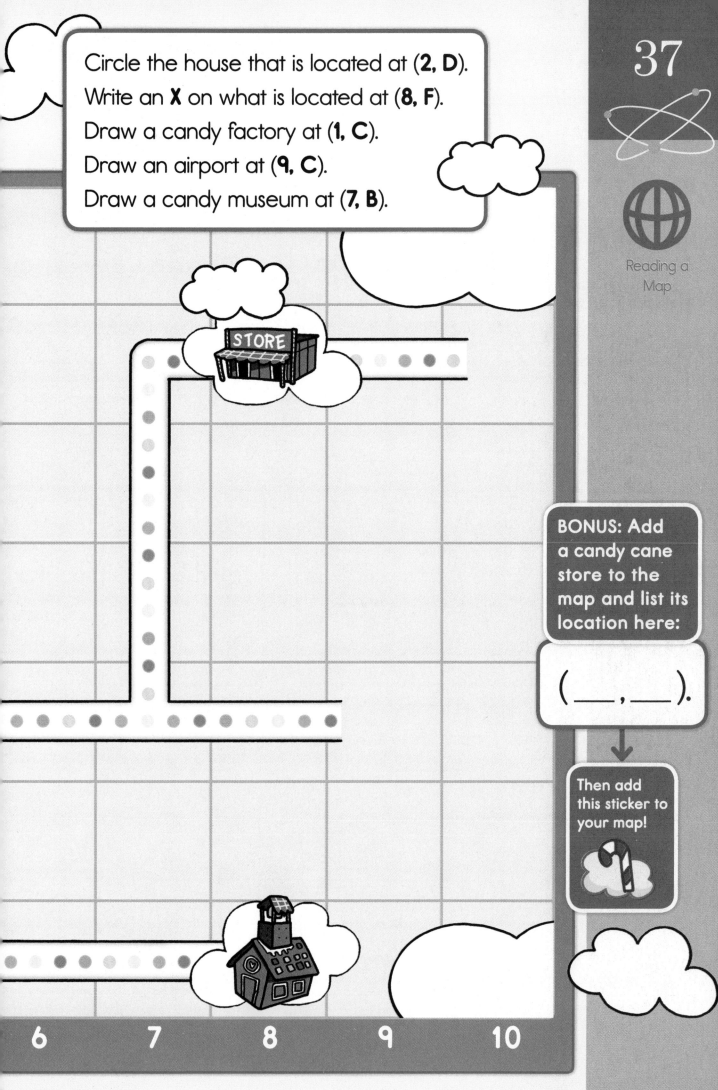

Circle the house that is located at (**2, D**).

Write an **X** on what is located at (**8, F**).

Draw a candy factory at (**1, C**).

Draw an airport at (**9, C**).

Draw a candy museum at (**7, B**).

STORE

BONUS: Add
a candy cane
store to the
map and list its
location here:

(___ , ___).

Then add
this sticker to
your map!

6   7   8   9   10

Tens and Ones

Upon completion, add this sticker to your path on the map!

Gingerbread House

Add the decorations to the gingerbread house. Add the groups to make 10. Then add more. Write the sum.

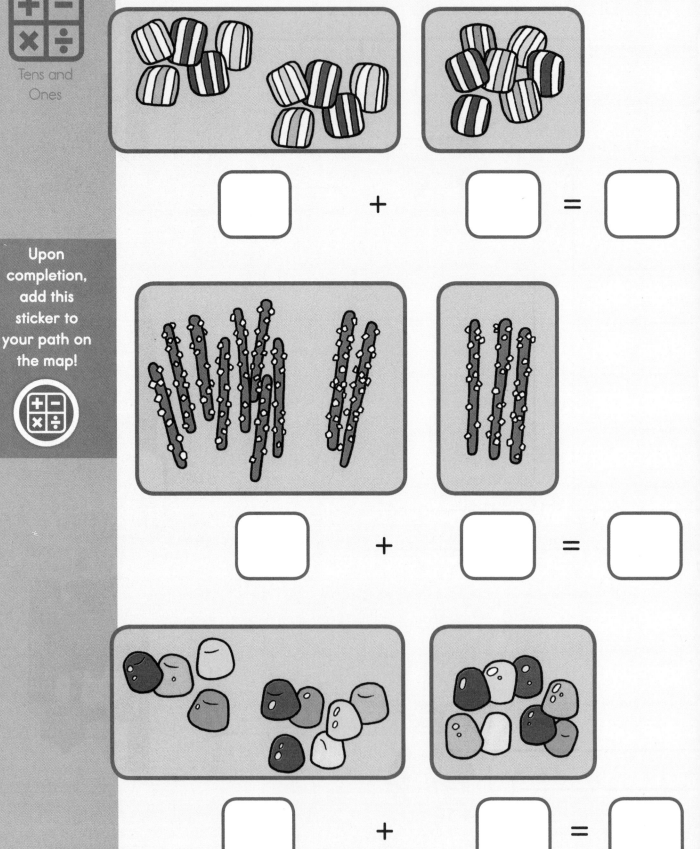

□ + □ = □

□ + □ = □

□ + □ = □

Changing Weather

Plants, trees, and other elements in nature change through the four seasons. Draw how each scene changes based on the season.

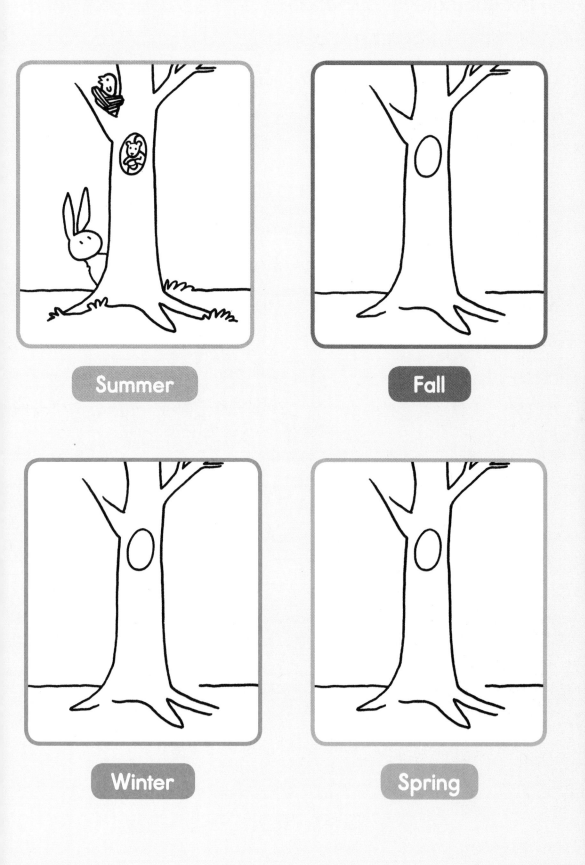

Summer

Fall

Winter

Spring

Upon completion, add this sticker to your path on the map!

The Fox and the Stork

Read the story. Write each **bold** word on the correct card.

The fox got an idea to trick the stork. The fox **asked** the stork to dinner. He **made** soup in a low bowl. The stork, with his long beak, could not **take** a sip! But the fox **drank** it up.

The stork did not get **angry**. He was **calm**. Instead, the stork invited the fox to dinner. He served fish in a **tall** vase. The fox, with his short snout, could not eat dinner. But the stork used his beak and **ate** it up. The fox got **mad**. It is not nice to **play** tricks!

SHORT A WORDS

asked

_____   _____   _____

_____   _____   _____

LONG A WORDS

_____   _____

_____   _____

Read aloud the words in the maze. Then follow the path with **short a** words to help the stork reach his dinner.

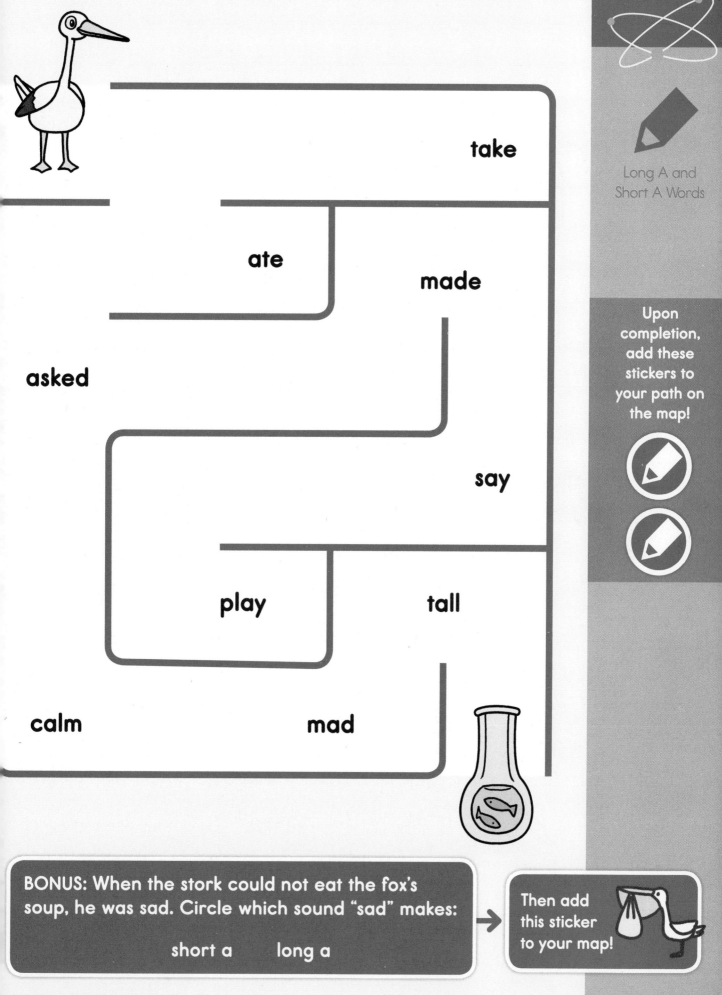

take

ate

made

asked

say

play   tall

calm   mad

Upon completion, add these stickers to your path on the map!

BONUS: When the stork could not eat the fox's soup, he was sad. Circle which sound "sad" makes:

short a   long a

Then add this sticker to your map!

Addition and Subtraction

What's Missing?

Fill in the missing number. Then use your answers and the corresponding letter to decode the riddle.

L $11 - 5 =$ ___

I ___ $+ 8 = 16$

U $12 -$ ___ $= 9$

R $8 +$ ___ $= 12$

N ___ $= 9 + 8$

G $9 + 9 =$ ___

Y $14 - 5 =$ ___

W ___ $= 6 + 9$

B $16 -$ ___ $= 6$

A $10 +$ ___ $= 15$

Why was Cinderella so good at dodge ball?

Because she was always

4	3	17	17	8	17	18

| | | | | from the
|---|---|---|---|
| 5 | 15 | 5 | 9 |

10	5	6	6

Addition and Subtraction

Upon completion, add these stickers to your path on the map!

Poetry

Read the poem and answer the questions.

Poetry and
Comprehension

A Little Mushroom House

I see a little mushroom house
with spots upon the roof.

I wonder who might live there now.
A turtle, frog, or two?

I see a tiny door and window,
made for someone small.

The closer I get, the more I must know!
Who's inside these walls?

I'll take a peek inside and look.
Oh! A teeny-tiny mouse!

She's by the fire with a book,
snug inside her mushroom house.

Which character in the poem lives inside the house?

The _____ lives

inside the house.

What is the setting of the poem?

The poem takes place

by a _____ .

Where can you look to see inside the house?

You can look in the

_____

_____ .

Could an elephant
live in the house?
Why or why not?
Write or draw your
answer.

Upon
completion,
add these
stickers to
your path on
the map!

A Feather in Your Cap

Puss in Boots buys bunches of feathers for his hat.
Count the number of tens. Write the number.

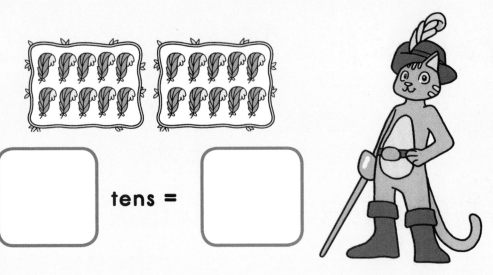

tens =

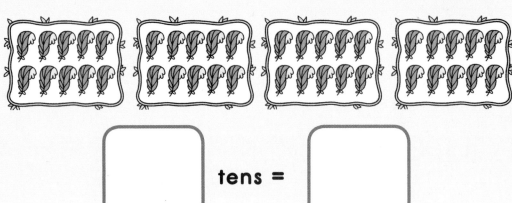

tens =

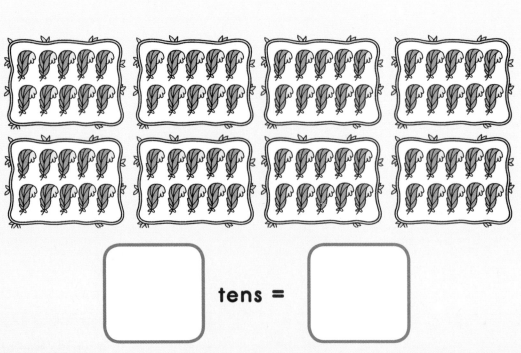

tens =

Level 3 complete!

Add this achievement sticker
to your path…

…and move on to

Level
4!

Animal
Survival

All You Can Eat

Some animals need to catch food to survive. Draw the correct amount of lines so each animal catches all of its food.

Help the squirrel eat the acorn in **3** lines.
Help the frog eat all the flies in **4** lines.
Help the bat eat all the mosquitoes in **5** lines.
Help the snake eat all the mice in **5** lines.
Help the duck eat all the worms in **6** lines.

Upon completion, add this sticker to your path on the map!

BONUS: People need to eat food to survive, too! Write or draw your favorite food.

Then add this sticker to your map!

Flying Flags

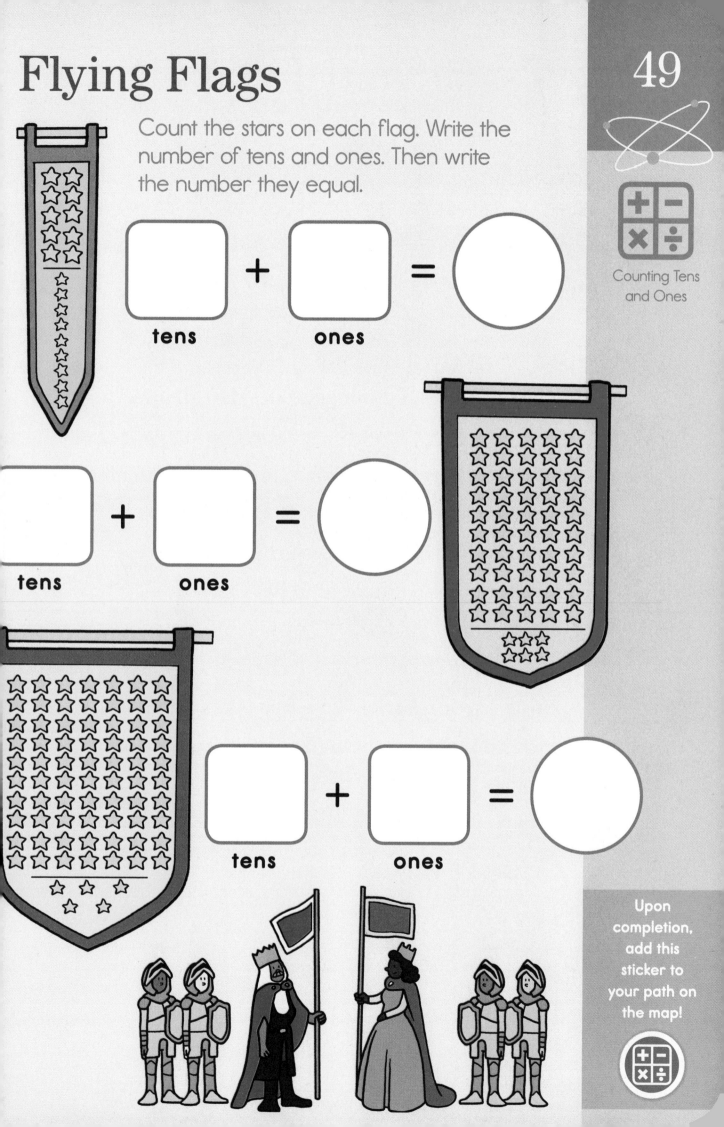

Count the stars on each flag. Write the number of tens and ones. Then write the number they equal.

Counting Tens and Ones

[ ] tens + [ ] ones = ( )

[ ] tens + [ ] ones = ( )

[ ] tens + [ ] ones = ( )

Upon completion, add this sticker to your path on the map!

Tricks and Treats

Long E and
Short E
Words

The Gingerbread Man

A little old woman wanted to **eat** a gingerbread cookie. So she made a gingerbread man and put him in the **oven** to bake. But the gingerbread  man came alive and jumped out! **He** ran away and yelled, "Don't eat **me**!" Soon an **elk** and a **hen** chased him, too. But no one could catch him. He was **free**! He **reached** a lake, and he couldn't swim. A fox **agreed** to **help** him across if the gingerbread man climbed up his **neck** and onto his back. They swam to the middle of the lake, but the fox was playing a trick! The fox tossed him in the air and caught him in his mouth. And that was the **end** of the gingerbread man.

SHORT E WORDS

oven

_____

_____

_____

_____

_____

LONG E WORDS

eat

_____   _____

_____   _____

_____   _____

Read aloud the words in the maze. Then follow the path with **long e** words to help free the gingerbread man.

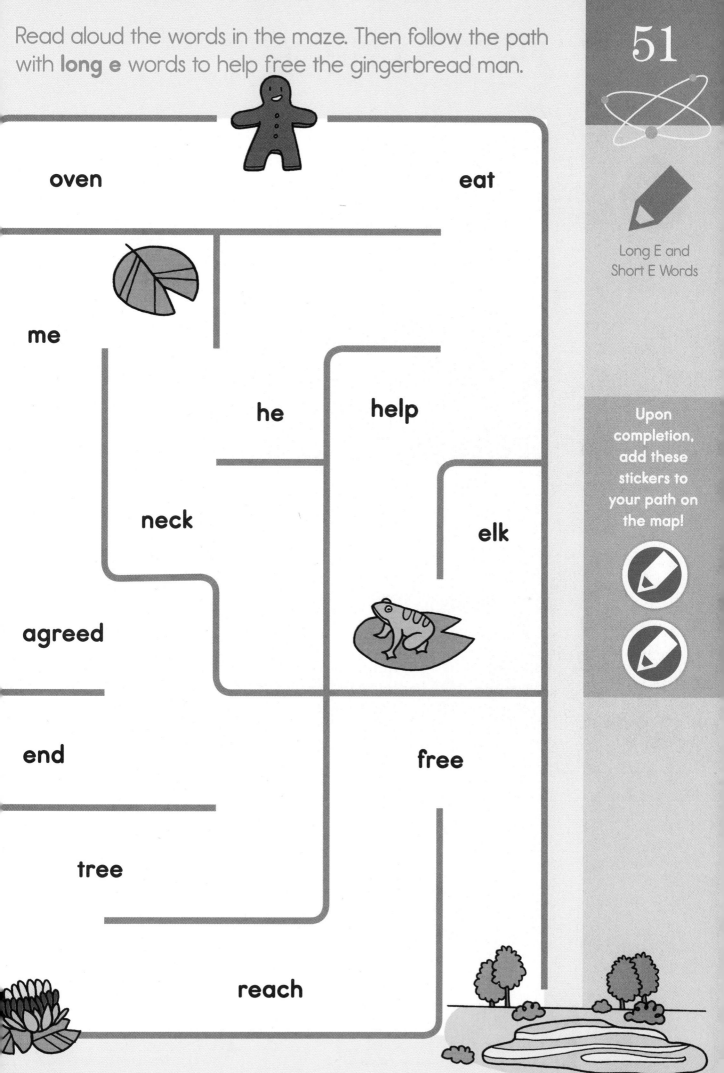

oven

eat

me

he

help

neck

elk

agreed

end

free

tree

reach

Long E and Short E Words

Upon completion, add these stickers to your path on the map!

Here to Help

Write whether each character offers goods or a service.

Little Pig builds homes.

Little Bo-Peep herds sheep.

The shoemaker makes shoes.

The baker bakes bread.

Mister Geppetto takes care of Pinocchio.

Betty Botter makes batter and cookies.

Draw or write about goods that you make or a service you do to help your community or family.

Goods and Services

Upon completion, add these stickers to your path on the map!

Brain Box

In a community, there are many jobs. Some people sell **goods**, which are things people make or grow. Others offer **services**, which are actions that help people.

Counting

Clever as a Fox

Match the number of tens and ones to the numbers on the right.

Upon completion, add these stickers to your path on the map!

TENS	ONES
1	8

TENS	ONES
7	6

TENS	ONES
5	7

TENS	ONES
2	9

TENS	ONES
8	6

TENS	ONES
4	2

TENS	ONES
6	1

TENS	ONES
2	2

TENS	ONES
3	4

TENS	ONES
9	5

18

61

95

22

Counting

57

86

42

34

BONUS:
The fox fooled 10 animals. Then it fooled 10 more animals. Later, it fooled 4 more animals. How many animals did the fox fool altogether?

_____ **animals**

Then add this sticker to your map!

29

76

That Cat

Complete each word with a letter from the box.

h	c	r
p	m	b

__at

__at

__at

WELCOME

__at

__at

__at

Word Family: -at

Write a sentence about what Puss in Boots might do next. Include two words from the cards above.

Level 4 complete!

Add this achievement sticker
to your path...

...and move on to

Level

5!

Who Lives in a Shoe?

Read the poem. Then circle the verbs.

Verbs

The Old Woman Who Lived in a Shoe

I saw an old woman,

Who lived in a shoe.

She had so many children,

And loved them all, too.

So she opened the oven,

And gave them all bread.

Then she kissed them all gladly,

And sent them to bed.

Write the past, present, and future tense of each verb.

She _____. He _____. He will eat.

    past   **present**   **future**

He slept. She _____. She _____.

    past   **present**   **future**

Write a verb that describes
what each child is doing.

Verbs

Upon
completion,
add these
stickers to
your path on
the map!

Compare

Magic Wands

Read the spinners of tens and ones and write each number. Then compare the numbers and write if they are less than (<) or greater than (>) each other.

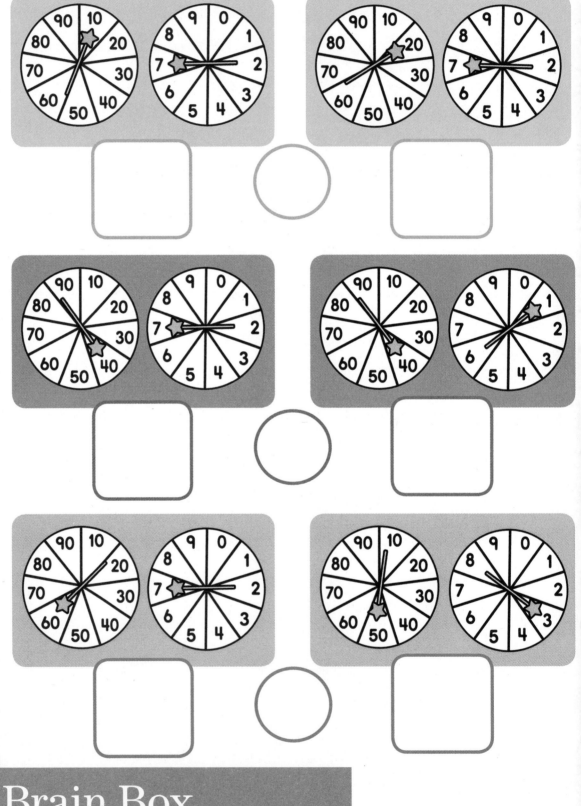

Brain Box

The symbol < means "less than." The symbol > means "greater than."

The symbol = means "equals" or "is the same as."

Spreading Fairy Dust

Tinker Bell is spreading fairy dust so some animals can fly! Help Tinker Bell find the correct animal by following directions.

Land Features

Upon completion, add this sticker to your path on the map!

Circle the animal on the hill.

Cross out the animal in front of the cliff.

Underline the animal next to the cave.

BONUS: Circle the name of the animal on the ice:

seal   polar bear

Then add this sticker to your map!

Flying Transportation

Each unicorn flies 10 more miles than each horse runs.
How many miles does each unicorn fly? Write the sum.

10 + 10 =

20 + 10 =

70 + 10 =

50 + 10 =

Each unicorn flies 10 fewer miles than each dragon. How many miles does each unicorn fly? Write the difference.

80 − 10 =

60 − 10 =

40 − 10 =

50 − 10 =

Upon completion, add these stickers to your path on the map!

64

Classifying
Materials

Jack and Jill

Read the poem. Then draw a line to match each object to the material it is made of.

Jack and Jill went up the hill

To fetch a pail of water.

Jack fell down and broke his crown,

And Jill came tumbling after.

plastic   gold   cotton   stone   wood

Circle the correct material.

Circle the material that is **brighter**.

black shirt

red jacket

Classifying
Materials

Circle the material that is **softer**.

grass

rocks

Upon
completion,
add these
stickers to
your path on
the map!

Circle the material that is **smoother**.

metal   **rope**

Circle the material that is **more absorbent**.

sponge   **paper**

Word Family: -en

Upon completion, add this sticker to your path on the map!

Dreaming Children

Complete each word with a letter or letters from the box.

_en

10

_en

_en

__en

_en

_en

t	d	m
h	op	p

Write a sentence about one of the children who lives in the shoe. Include two words from the beds above.

Little Red Riding Hood

Circle the units of time you would use to measure each event.

Time

Little Red Riding Hood was born and grew into a little girl.

years   **weeks**

She baked a cake for her grandmother.

months   **hours**

She picked flowers for her grandmother.

minutes   **years**

Then she walked a few miles to her grandmother's house.

seconds   **hours**

The Big Bad Wolf knocked on Grandmother's door.

weeks   **seconds**

Little Red Riding Hood saw the wolf and gasped!

seconds   **years**

Upon completion, add this sticker to your path on the map!

BONUS: Write these words in order from the shortest amount of time to the longest: months, days, years, minutes, hours, weeks.

_____ → _____ → _____
Shortest

_____ → _____ → _____
Longest

Then add this sticker to your map!

Tinker Bell's Wink

Read the story. Write each **bold** word on the correct card.

Tinker Bell was a **tiny** fairy with a **bright smile**.

One day she went for a speedy **zip** in the sky.

She flew **high** and did a **flip**.

She took a **dip** and a **dive**.

How her fairy dust did **shine**!

With a happy **grin**, and a **little wink**, she flew home.

SHORT I WORDS

_____

_____

_____

_____

_____

LONG I WORDS

tiny
_____   _____

_____   _____

_____   _____

Follow the path with **long i** words to help Tinker Bell reach the moon.

Long I and Short I Words

Upon completion, add these stickers to your path on the map!

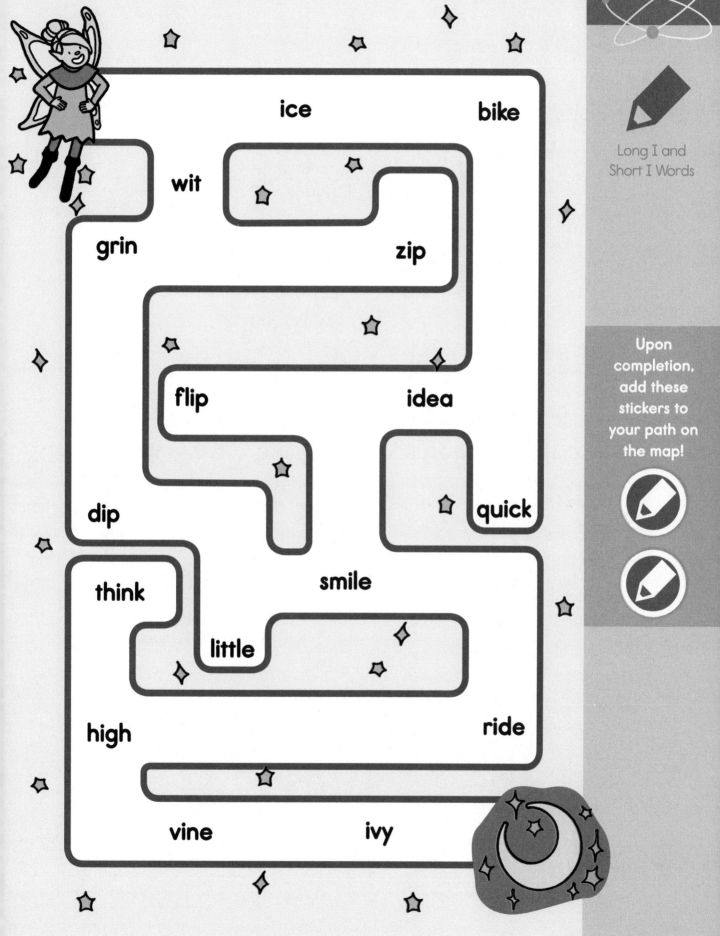

ice   bike

wit

grin   zip

flip   idea

dip   quick

smile

think

little

high   ride

vine   ivy

Measurement

Baby Bear's Bed

How many paw prints long is Baby Bear's bed?

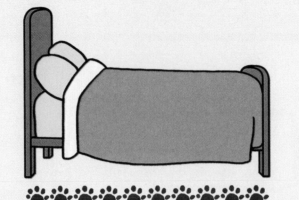

Measure with Baby Bear's paw.

Baby paws long

Measure with Mama Bear's paw.

Mama paws long

Measure with Papa Bear's paw.

Papa paws long

Level 5 complete!

Add this achievement sticker to your path...

...and move on to

Level 6!

Where in the World?

Use the compass and hints to label the continents and oceans.

CONTINENTS

Antarctica is the continent that is farthest south.

Australia is the smallest continent.

North America is the farthest west on the map.

South America is south of North America.

Asia is the largest continent.

Europe is to the west of Asia.

Africa is south of Europe.

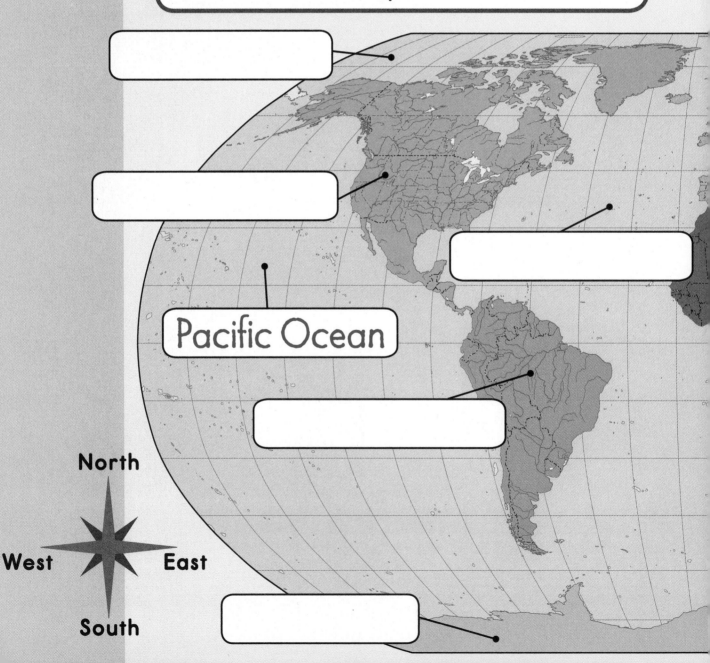

Pacific Ocean

North

West East

South

Continents and Oceans

OCEANS

The Arctic Ocean is the ocean farthest north.

The Southern Ocean is the farthest south.

The Atlantic Ocean is between South and North America and Africa.

The Indian Ocean is south of Asia.

The Pacific Ocean is west of North America and South America.

Upon completion, add these stickers to your path on the map!

Europe

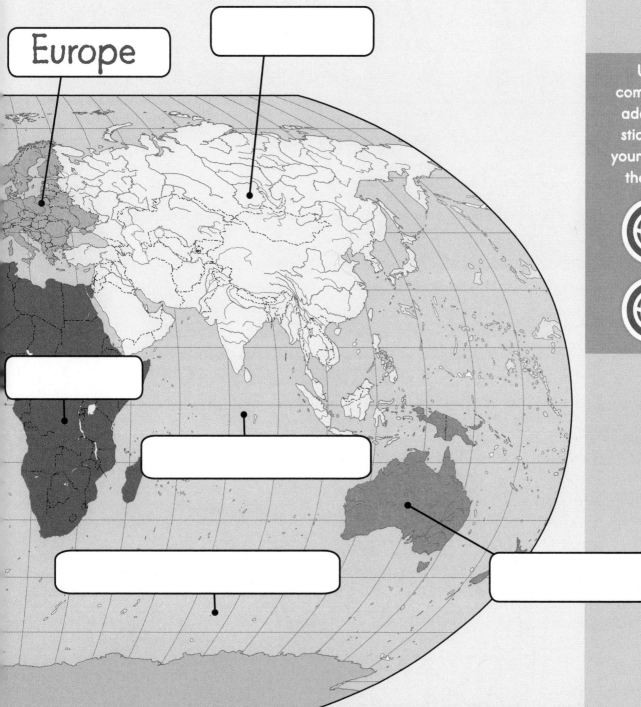

Word Family:
-in

Upon
completion,
add this
sticker to
your path on
the map!

Dragon Grin

Complete each word with a letter or letters
from the box.

sp	f	w
t	b	p

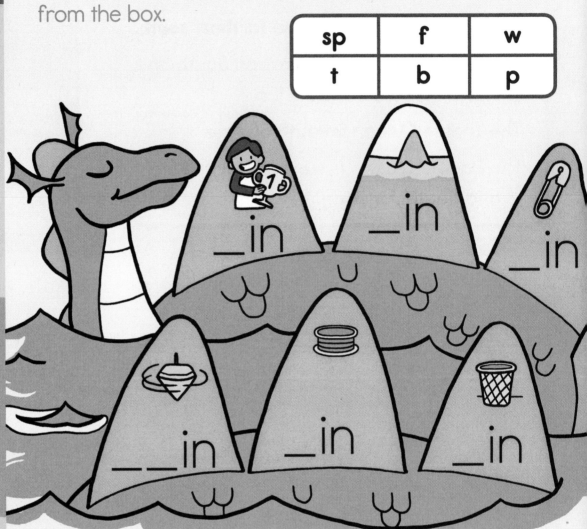

_in

_in

_in

__in

_in

_in

Write or draw what might make a dragon grin.

House of Straw

Circle the best estimate for the length of each object.

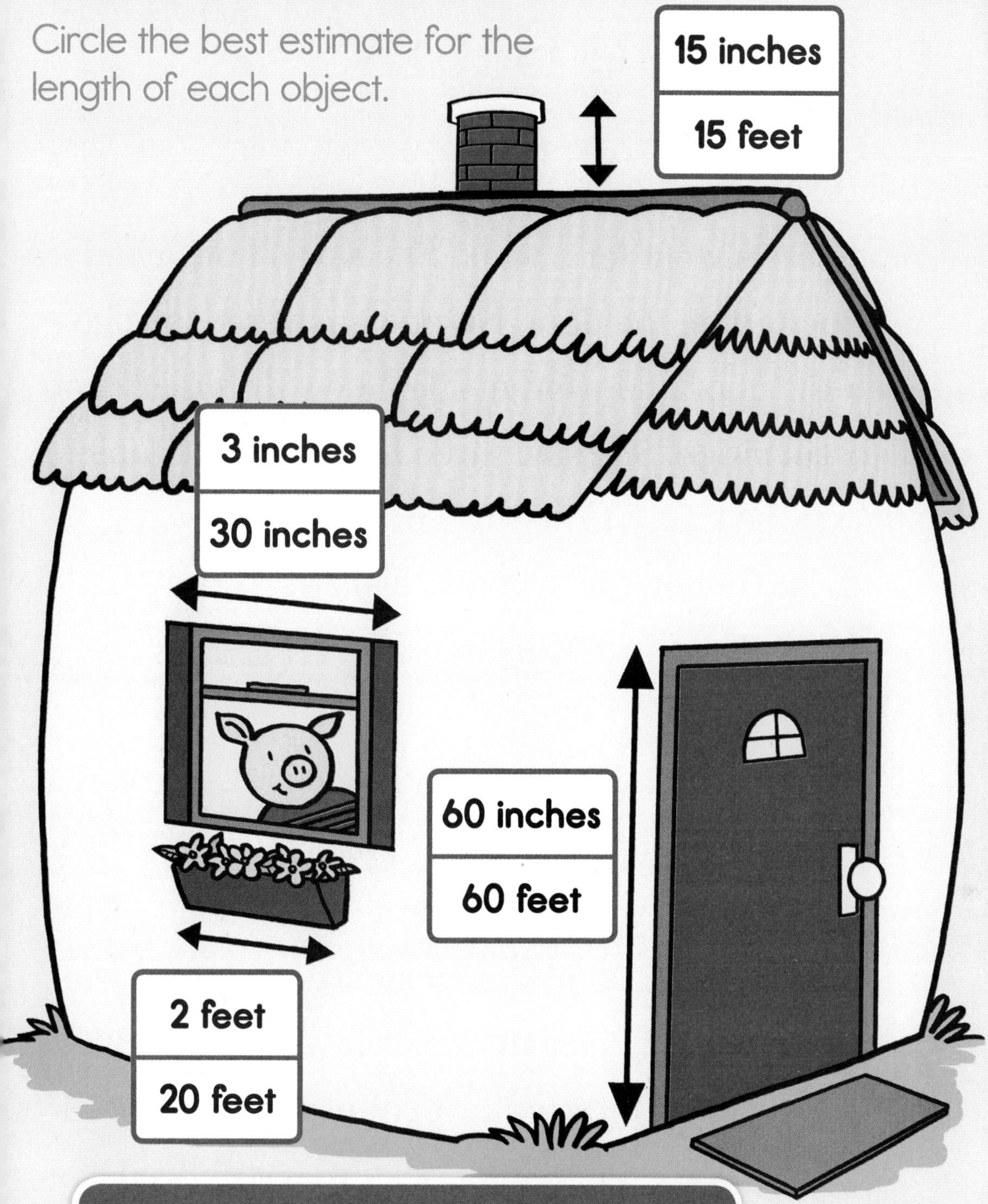

15 inches

15 feet

3 inches

30 inches

60 inches

60 feet

2 feet

20 feet

Upon completion, add this sticker to your path on the map!

BONUS: Can the width of the pig's straw house be both 10 feet long and 120 inches long? Why or why not?

Then add this sticker to your map!

Goldilocks and the Three Bears

Read the story. Write each **bold** word on the correct card.

Goldilocks went for a walk. She saw a house and **knocked** on the door. **No** one answered, **so** she **opened** the door and went inside. She was hungry and smelled **porridge**. She saw three **bowls on** the table. She tasted the first. "This is too **hot**!" she said. She tasted the second. "This is too **cold**!" The third was just right, so she ate it all.

She was tired and wanted to sit and rest. She saw three chairs. She sat in the first. "This is too **soft**!" she said. She sat in the second. "This feels like a **rock**!" The third was just right, so she sat down. But the chair **broke** into pieces!

Goldilocks was still tired, so she went upstairs to rest. Then, the three bears came **home**. "Someone ate my porridge," growled Papa Bear. "Someone broke my chair," growled Mama Bear. "And someone is in my bed!" yelled Baby Bear! Just then, Goldilocks **woke** up and saw the bears. She **hopped** out the window and ran all the way home!

Upon completion, add these stickers to your path on the map!

SHORT O WORDS

knocked

LONG O WORDS

no

Long O and Short O Words

Follow the paths with **short o** words to help Goldilocks reach the window.

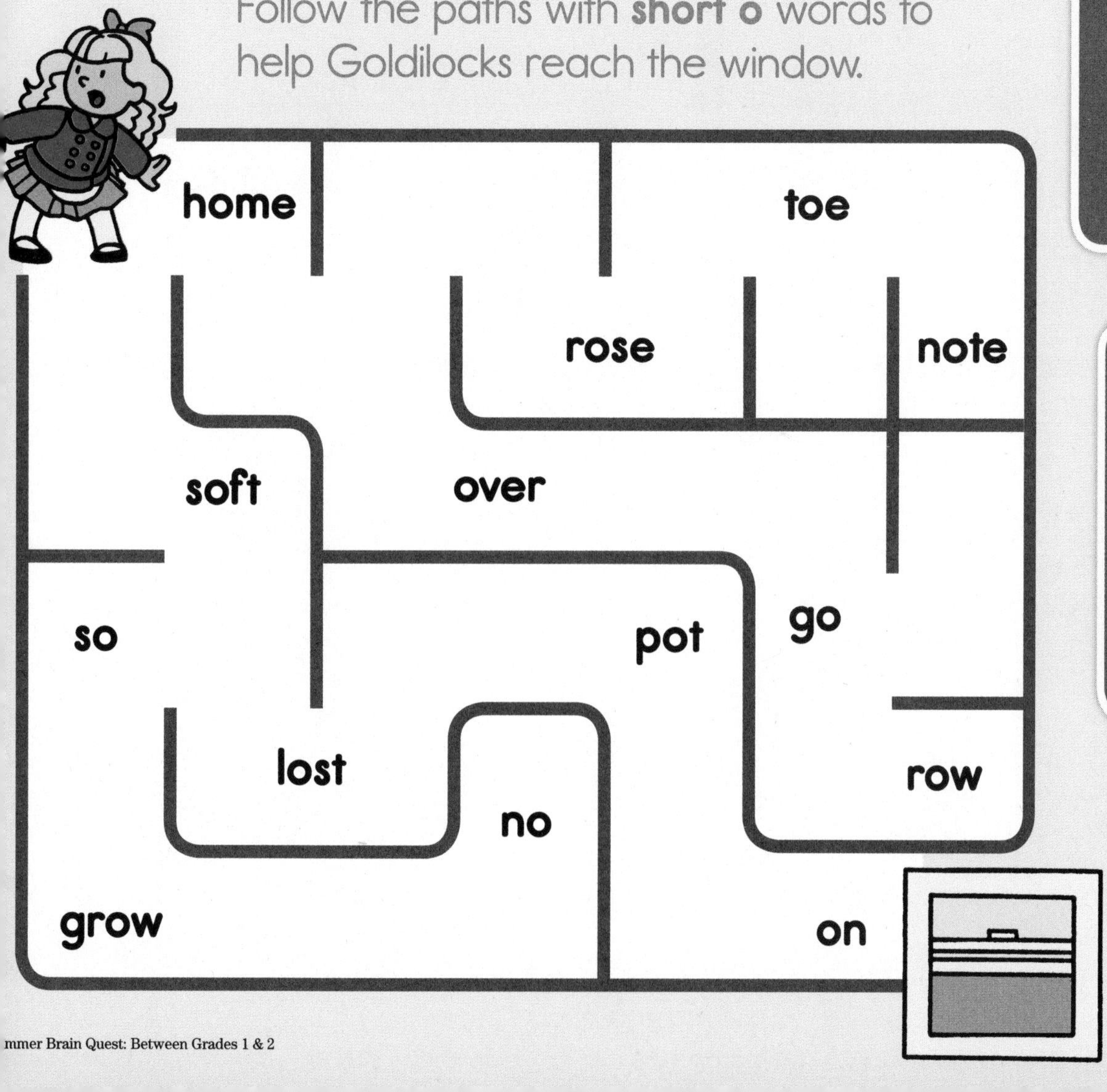

BONUS:
The bears fixed the oak chair. Circle which sound "oak" makes:

short o

long o

Then add this sticker to your map!

home   toe

rose   note

soft   over

so   pot   go

lost   row

no

grow   on

Plant Survival

Spreading Seeds

Read about how each animal moves seeds. Then draw a line to lead each animal through the maze to its seed and destination.

burrs

grass seeds

Brain Box

Plants grow roots and stay in one place. Animals can move around and help spread plants' seeds!

Birds eat fruits of plants. Birds digest the fruit and poop out the seeds while they fly to their nests.

Ants carry grass seeds and store them at their anthill so they can eat them later.

blackberry
seeds

BONUS:
What is another
animal, besides a
wolf, that could
carry burrs?
Write the name
of the animal.

Seeds often get
tangled in animal
fur or feathers and
then drop off the
animal later. **Wolves**
carry burrs in their
fur and drop them in the woods.

Then add
this sticker
to your map!

Wood Houses

These pigs have bundles of 10 sticks and single sticks to build each house. Draw the single sticks they need to add. Then write the number of sticks in all.

46 + 3 = _____ sticks in all

25 + 3 = _____ sticks in all

48 + 2 = _____ sticks in all

These pigs have too many sticks. Cross out the sticks each pig should chop up for firewood. Write the number of sticks left.

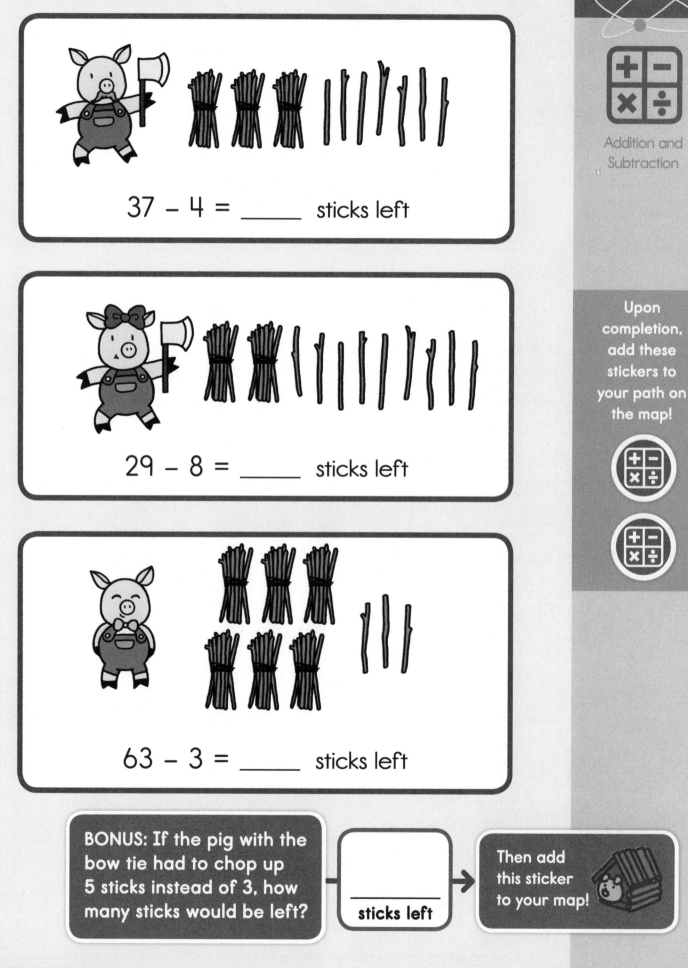

$37 - 4 =$ _____ sticks left

$29 - 8 =$ _____ sticks left

$63 - 3 =$ _____ sticks left

Upon completion, add these stickers to your path on the map!

BONUS: If the pig with the bow tie had to chop up 5 sticks instead of 3, how many sticks would be left?

_____ sticks left

Then add this sticker to your map!

Builder's Maze

The pigs need supplies to build their houses. Draw a line through the maze by choosing each path that has a noun.

Brain Box

A **noun** is a word that names a person, place, or thing.

ladder

climb

strong

wires

CEMENT

careful

fix

hammer

nails

lift

BONUS: Write two sentences describing each pig's house. Use one noun from the maze in each sentence.

Nouns

Then add this sticker to your map!

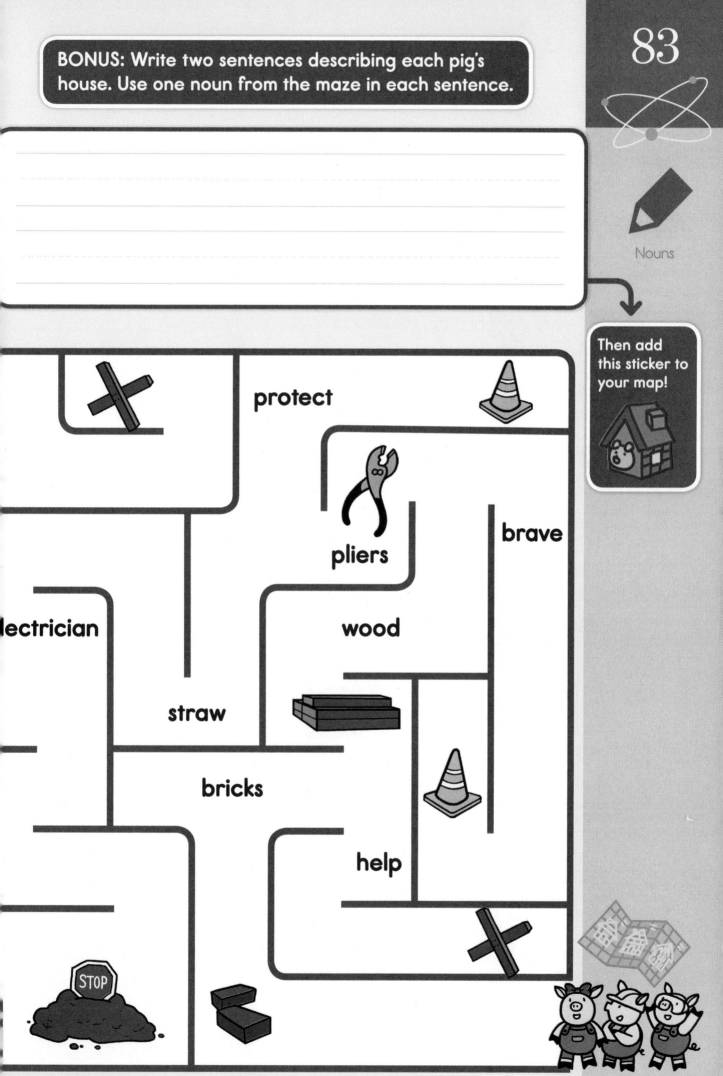

protect

pliers

brave

electrician

wood

straw

bricks

help

STOP

Habitat
Diversity

Upon
completion,
add this
sticker to
your path on
the map!

Animals All Over the World

Read about each animal. Then draw a line to match each animal to its habitat.

A **fennec fox** digs in the sand and sleeps underground to stay cool during hot days.

Rain Forest

Some types of algae grow on **sloth** hair to help a sloth blend into trees and hide in plain sight.

Desert

A **turban snail** tucks into its shell to stay wet during low tide.

Arctic

A **musk ox** grows long hollow hair to stay warm.

Grassland

A **Masai giraffe** has a blue-black tongue that won't get sunburned while eating.

Tidepool

Fishing for Stars

To catch the stars, write the sum.

Addition and Subtraction

Upon completion, add this sticker to your path on the map!

47
+ 20
_____

47
+ 30
_____

47
+ 40
_____

25
+ 50
_____

25
+ 60
_____

25
+ 70
_____

34
+ 20
_____

34
+ 30
_____

34
+ 40
_____

Addition and
Subtraction

Subtracting Stars

To catch the stars, write the difference.

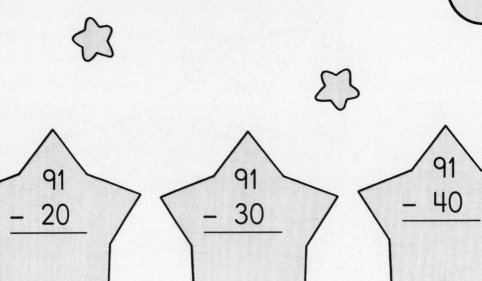

$$91 - 20$$ $$91 - 30$$ $$91 - 40$$

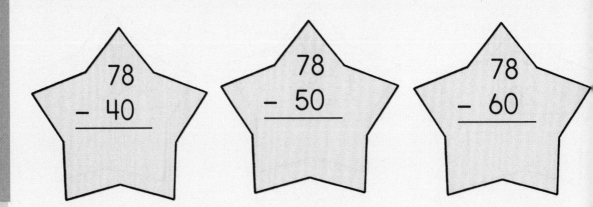

$$78 - 40$$ $$78 - 50$$ $$78 - 60$$

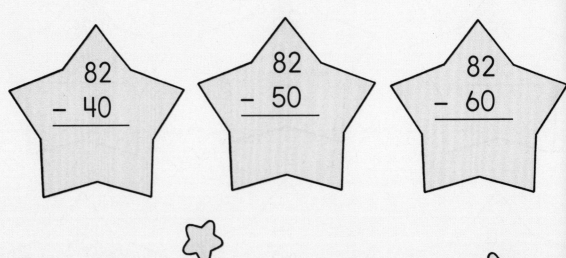

$$82 - 40$$ $$82 - 50$$ $$82 - 60$$

Level 6 complete!

Add this achievement sticker
to your path…

…and move on to

Level
7!

Feed the Dragon

Color each picture that shows the dragon rider using natural resources to meet his needs, and the dragon's, too!

Brain Box

A **natural resource** is something that can be found in nature, including air, water, sunlight, plants, animals, minerals, and more. People use natural resources to meet their basic needs for food, clothing, and shelter.

Magic Carpet

Which of the shapes are closed? Color the carpets with closed shapes.

Shapes

Upon completion, add this sticker to your path on the map!

Draw five different closed shapes on the carpet. Then color them.

Fly Away with Mother Goose

Read the story. Write each **bold** word on the correct card.

Long U and Short U Words

Jump on! With Mother Goose we'll fly.

On **up** to the stars **through** the **true blue** sky.

Hear the **music**, **hum** the cat's **tune**.

With any **luck**, we'll soon reach the moon.

We'll fly **under** the cow,

to the golden **sun**.

Flying with Mother Goose

is rhyming **fun**!

SHORT U WORDS

jump _____ _____ _____

_____ _____ _____

LONG U WORDS

_____ _____ _____

_____ _____

Follow the paths with **short u** words to help Mother Goose reach the sun.

Long U and Short U Words

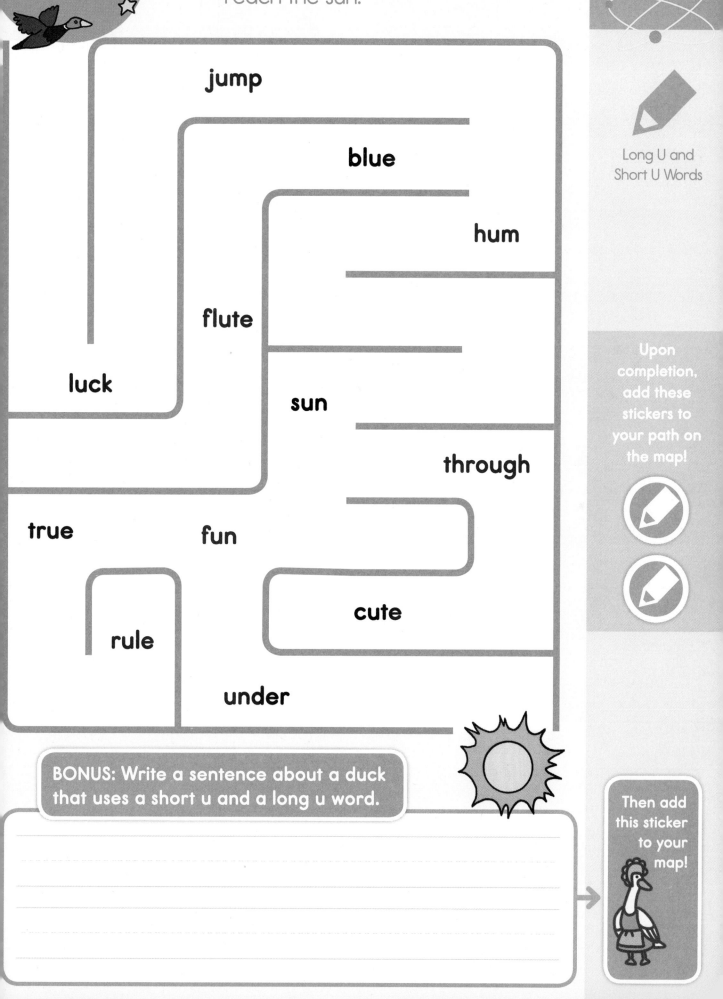

jump

blue

hum

flute

luck

sun

through

true

fun

cute

rule

under

Upon completion, add these stickers to your path on the map!

BONUS: Write a sentence about a duck that uses a short u and a long u word.

Then add this sticker to your map!

Shapes

Upon completion, add this sticker to your path on the map!

My Own Castle

Draw a castle using each shape at least once.

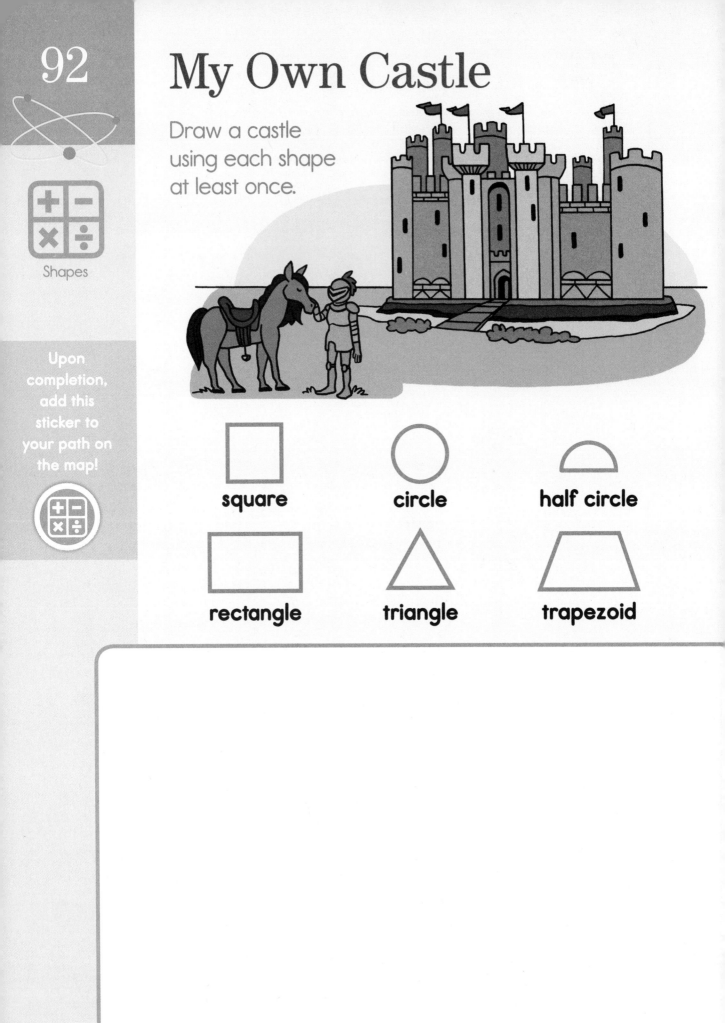

square

circle

half circle

rectangle

triangle

trapezoid

Travel Through the Desert

Read the map key and follow the directions to draw a map.

Making a Map

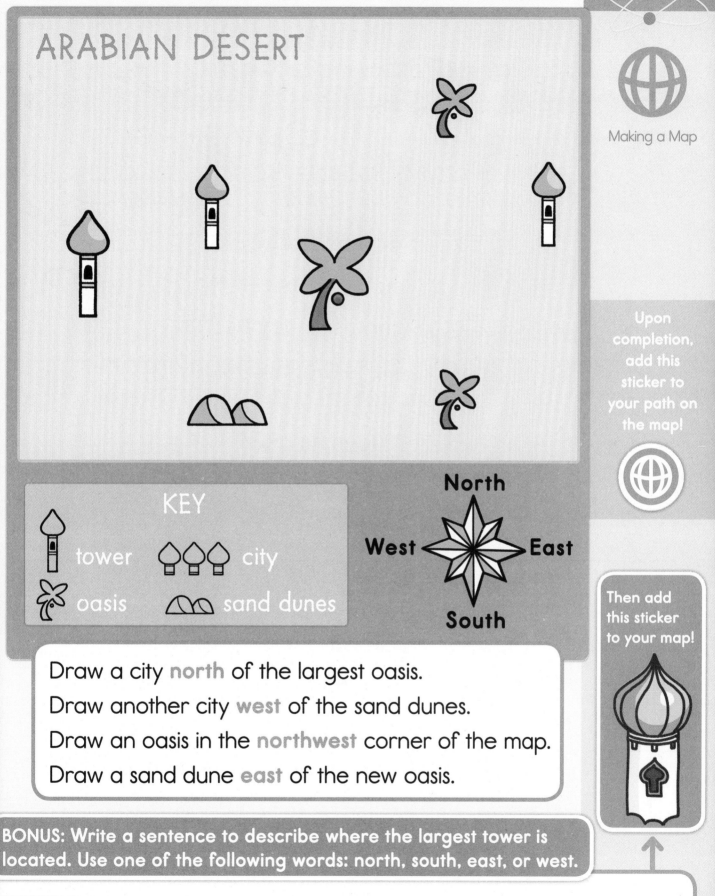

ARABIAN DESERT

KEY

tower   city

oasis   sand dunes

North

West   **East**

South

Draw a city **north** of the largest oasis.

Draw another city **west** of the sand dunes.

Draw an oasis in the **northwest** corner of the map.

Draw a sand dune **east** of the new oasis.

BONUS: Write a sentence to describe where the largest tower is located. Use one of the following words: north, south, east, or west.

Upon completion, add this sticker to your path on the map!

Then add this sticker to your map!

Use Your Five Senses

Read the poem and answer the questions.

The Sleepy Dragon

See the tired dragon in the sky?

He looks at you with his red eye.

He opens his mouth to try to roar,

But all you hear is the loudest snore!

Is he hungry? Does he need a snack?

There's juicy fruit in your backpack.

Call to him and hold it high!

He turns to you and starts to fly.

As he gets closer, his nostrils flare.

Sour black smoke fills the air.

Give his rugged snout a tap.

He'll gulp the fruit, then take a nap.

What things can you touch in the poem?

What things can you see in the poem?

Poetry and Comprehension

What things can you hear in the poem?

Upon completion, add these stickers to your path on the map!

What things can you smell in the poem?

What things can you taste in the poem?

Fractions

Rare Birds

These rare birds make nests divided into halves (2 equal parts). Color one-half of each nest.

These rare birds make nests divided into fourths
(4 equal parts). Color one-fourth of each nest.

Upon
completion,
add these
stickers to
your path on
the map!

BONUS: The firebird has
beautiful red feathers.
Is the feather shaded in
halves? Explain your answer.

Then add
this sticker
to your map!

Word Family:
-it

Upon
completion,
add this
sticker to
your path on
the map!

Flitting Feathers

Complete each word with
a letter from the box.

f	h	k
l	p	s

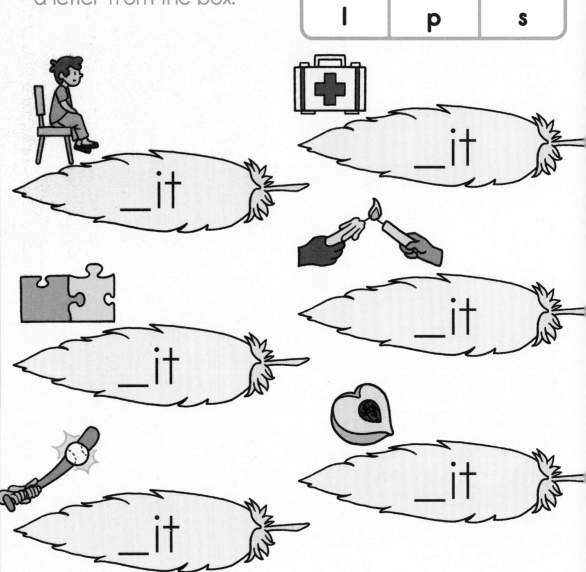

_it

_it

_it

_it

_it

_it

A firebird has feathers that look like they are lit on fire.
Write a sentence to describe the colors.

Castle Communities

Label each area as rural, suburban, or urban.

Rural,
Suburban,
and Urban
Communities

_____

Upon
completion,
add this
sticker to
your path on
the map!

_____

Brain Box

People live in different types of communities. **Rural** communities have lots of open space, like farmland, and people are spread out. **Suburban** communities have less open space and more people. In **urban** communities like cities, houses, people, and businesses are close together.

_____

Bodies of
Water

The Thirsty Dragon

Label each body of water in the space below.

Brain Box

There are different types of
bodies of water. A **sea** is a large
body of salt water. A **river** is a
flow of water that crosses land.
A **waterfall** is a river that falls
down from a high place. A **lake**
is water that is surrounded by
land. A **pond** is also water that
is surrounded by land, but it is
smaller than a lake.

sea   river   waterfall   lake   pond

Bodies of Water

Upon completion, add these stickers to your path on the map!

BONUS: What is the closest body of water near you? Draw or write about the body of water.

Then add this sticker to your map!

Time

Fairy-Tale Time

It's time to wake up! Draw the hands on each clock to show when each character wakes up.

Little Boy Blue wakes up at 7:00.

Robin Hood wakes up at 8:15.

Mary and her lamb wake up at 9:30.

Sleeping Beauty wakes up at 10:45.

It's time for lunch! Read the clock. Then write the time when each character has lunch.

Time

Upon completion, add these stickers to your path on the map!

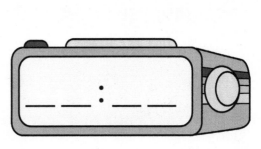

_ _ _ : _ _

_ _ _ : _ _

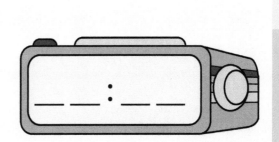

_ _ _ : _ _

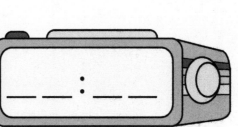

_ _ _ : _ _

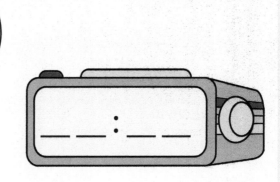

Word Family:
-ot

Upon completion, add this sticker to your path on the map!

Jot a Lot

Complete each word with a letter or letters from the box.

kn	h	d
c	t	p

_ _ot

_ _ot

_ _ot

_ _ _ot

_ _ot

_ _ot

Write or draw what you think the knight forgot.

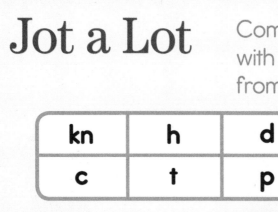

Level 7 complete!

Add this achievement sticker
to your path…

…and move on to
Level 8!

Man-Made
Features and
Communities

Helping Hand

Draw each item to help these communities.

bridge

dock

Brain Box

People make
changes to their
environment.
They build
**man-made
structures** and
other features to
help meet their
basic needs.

power lines

park

At the Fair

Which is the correct coin? Draw a line from the coin to the item you can buy with it.

Upon completion, add this sticker to your path on the map!

Changing Forms

The wizard is organizing his lab. Draw a line to match each form of water to the correct box. Then draw other solids, liquids, and gases in the boxes.

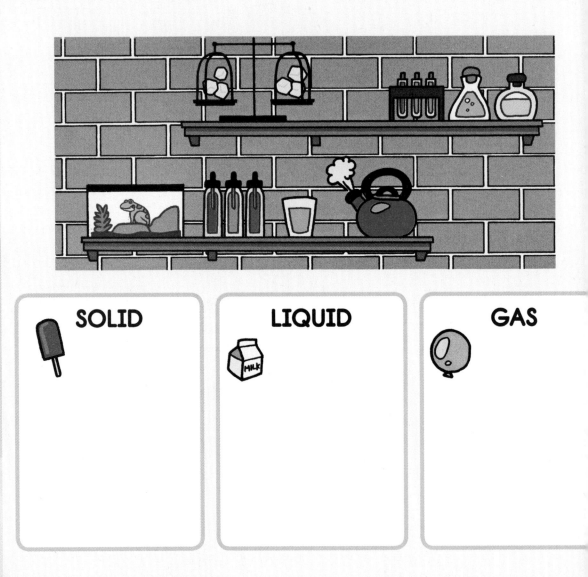

SOLID	LIQUID	GAS

Label each form of water as a solid, liquid, or gas.

_____ _____ _____

Summer Brain Quest: Between Grades 1 &

Upon completion, add this sticker to your path on the map!

Brain Box

Matter can exist as a **solid, liquid,** or **gas.** Water can exist as a solid (ice), liquid (water), or gas (steam) based on its temperature!

Out in the Storm

Write the name of each weather event.
Use the words from the boxes.

tornado	lightning	hail	fog

Weather

_____

_____

_____

_____

Upon completion, add this sticker to your path on the map!

Brain Box

A **tornado** is a funnel of very fast winds that touches the earth.

BONUS: In a lightning storm, what should the Courageous Lion do?

_____

Then add this sticker to your map!

Adventures in Oz

Fill in an adjective to complete each sentence.

A tornado picked up Dorothy's _____ house.

Dorothy is wearing

_____ shoes.

The Tin Man protects

his friends from the

_____ wolves.

The _____ Scarecrow scares away the wild crows.

The Lion lets out a _____ roar.

Dorothy clicks her _____ heels and returns home.

Money

Spare Parts

Help buy parts for the Tin Man. Write the amount of money each part costs.

= [___] ¢

= [___] ¢

Upon completion, add these stickers to your path on the map!

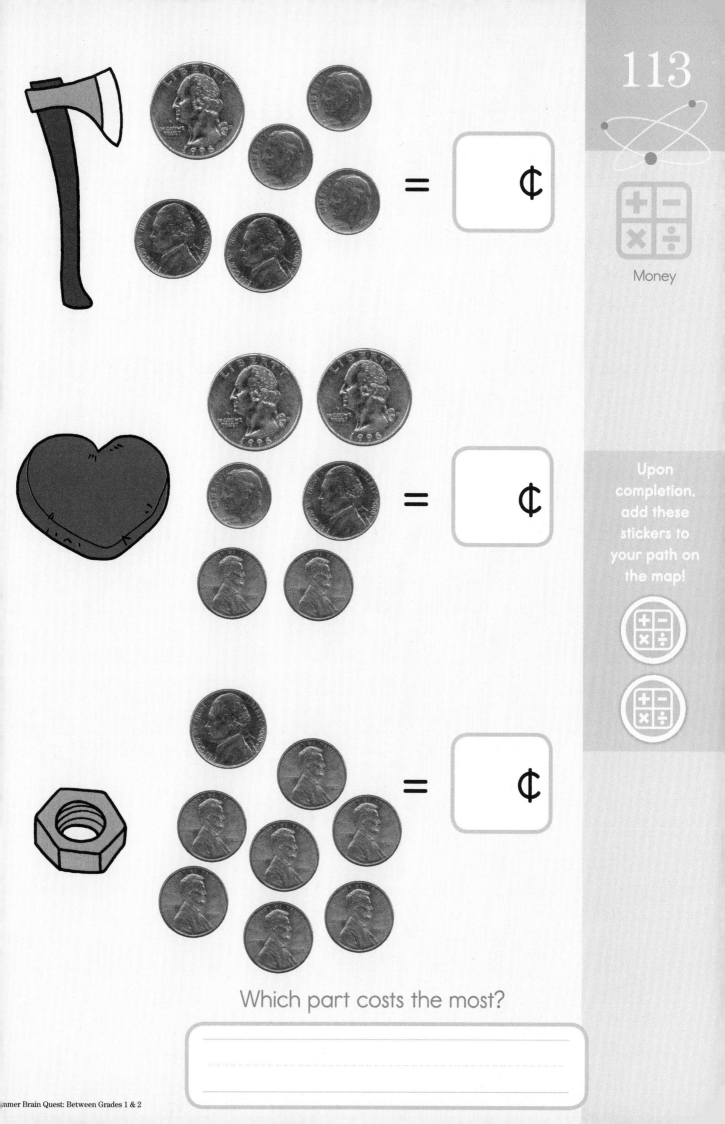

= ¢

= ¢

= ¢

Which part costs the most?

Word Family:
-ug

Tug!

Complete each word with a letter or letters from the box.

m	j	pl	b	h	r

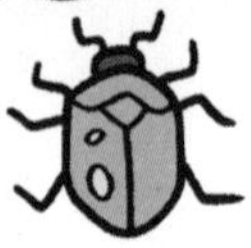

_ug

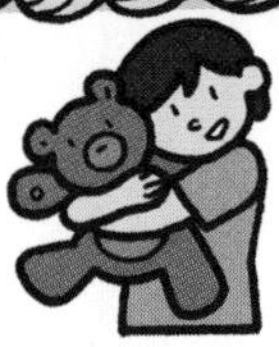

_ug

_ug

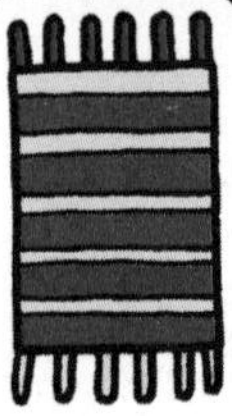

_ _ug

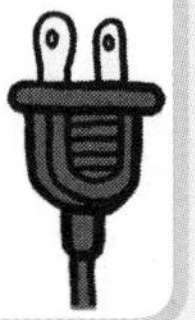

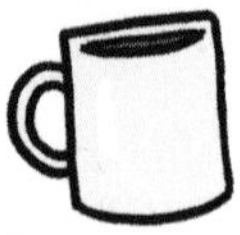

_ug

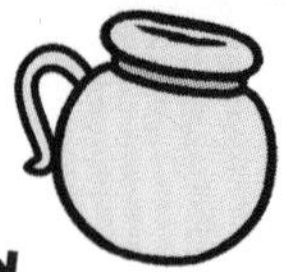

_ug

The prince gently tugs on Rapunzel's strong hair before he climbs it. Write or draw what happens when he reaches Rapunzel.

Upon completion, add this sticker to your path on the map!

Connect the Dots

Start at 10. Connect the dots in order to find the hidden picture. Then color it.

Counting

Upon completion, add this sticker to your path on the map!

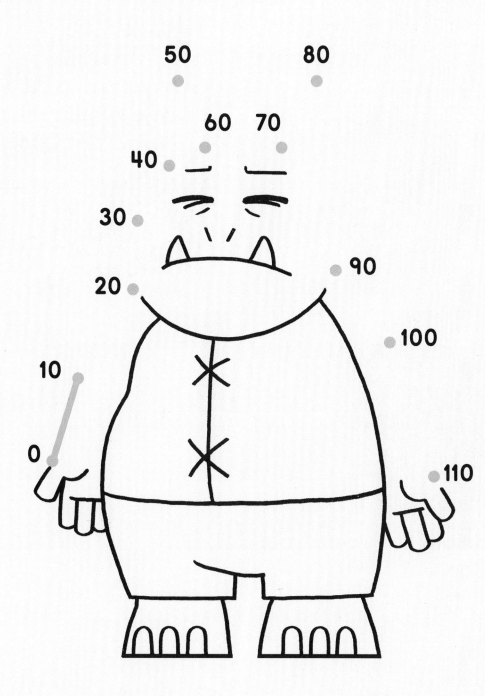

Fill in the missing numbers.

_____, 20, 30, _____, 50, 60, _____, _____, 90, _____

Oranges to Orange Juice

Start the maze at the arrow. Draw a line through the pictures in the correct order to show how oranges are made into orange juice.

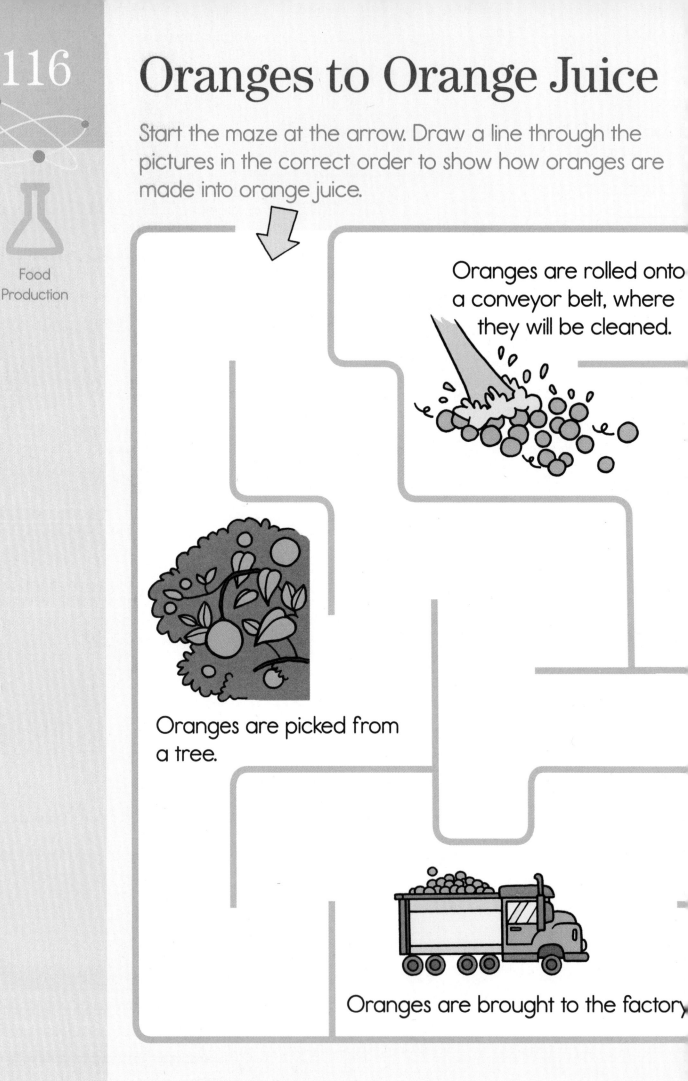

Oranges are rolled onto a conveyor belt, where they will be cleaned.

Oranges are picked from a tree.

Oranges are brought to the factory.

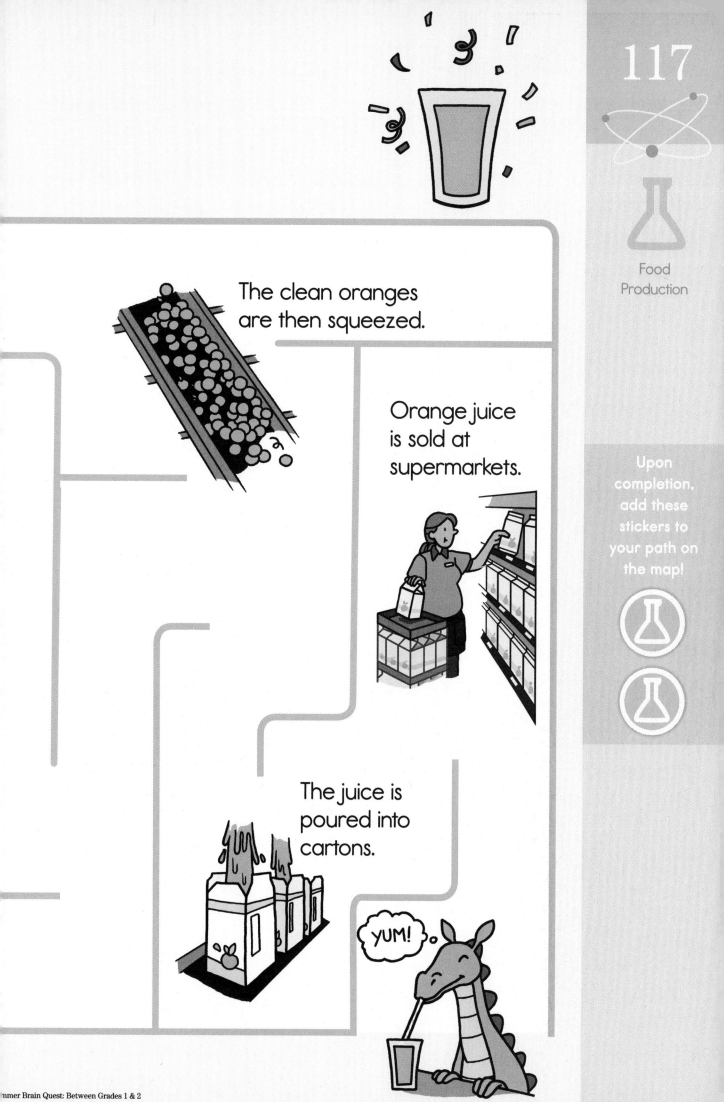

The clean oranges
are then squeezed.

Orange juice
is sold at
supermarkets.

Upon
completion,
add these
stickers to
your path on
the map!

The juice is
poured into
cartons.

YUM!

The Princess and the Pea

The queen, the prince, and the princess each need a punctuation mark to speak. Draw a line to match each punctuation mark to each character.

Punctuation

The queen wants to ask a question.

!

The prince is excited to talk to the princess.

.

The princess is telling a story.

?

Write in the correct punctuation mark at the end of each sentence.

Punctuation

The prince wants to marry a princess ____

A woman knocks at the door. Is she a real princess ____

The queen tests her by placing a pea under her mattress ____

The woman feels the pea. The prince is delighted—she is a real princess ____

The prince and princess get married ____

Moving on to Hundreds

Fill in each vehicle's number in the place-value chart.

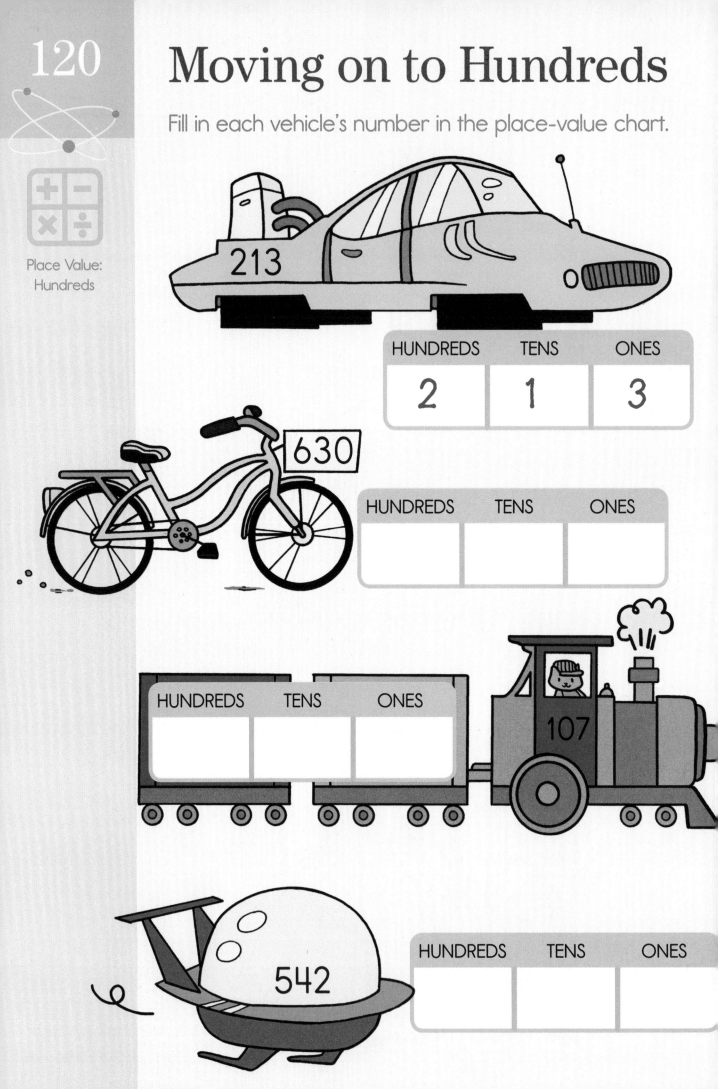

HUNDREDS	TENS	ONES
2	1	3

HUNDREDS	TENS	ONES

HUNDREDS	TENS	ONES

HUNDREDS	TENS	ONES

Place Value: Hundreds

121

Place Value:
Hundreds

HUNDREDS	TENS	ONES

Upon
completion,
add these
stickers to
your path on
the map!

HUNDREDS	TENS	ONES

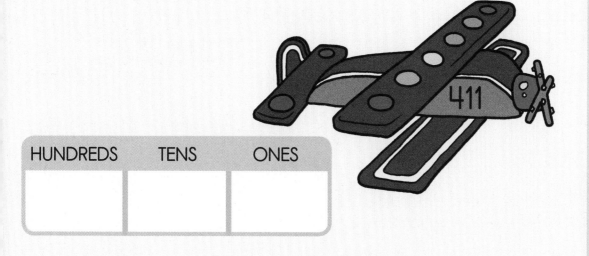

HUNDREDS	TENS	ONES

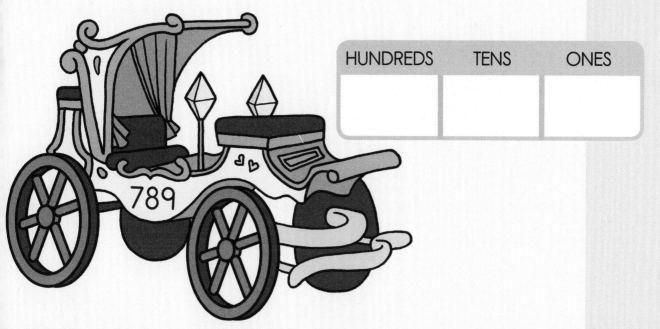

How Wind
and Water
Shape the
Earth

Save the Emerald City Castle!

Over time, wind and water are changing the land around the castle! Follow the instructions to help the environment and save the castle.

Brain Box

Erosion occurs when wind or water wears away soil and rocks.

A **flood** occurs when land that is usually dry is submerged underwater.

As the ocean tides move in and out, the land is eroding. To help stop erosion, draw some trees between the castle and the ocean.

Over time, the river is rising and may flood the castle. To help stop a flood, draw a dam in the river.

Wind is pushing the sand into dunes. To help prevent the creation of sand dunes, draw some beach grass to hold down the sand.

Where have you seen erosion?

Write or draw how wind and water change the land where you live.

How Wind and Water Shape the Earth

Upon completion, add these stickers to your path on the map!

CONGRATULATIONS!
You completed all of your science quests! You earned:

Princess Jewels

Follow the instructions to make princess crowns.

Color the jewels with a 5 in the ones place **purple**.
Color the jewels with a 7 in the tens place **green**.
Color the jewels with a 3 in the hundreds place **blue**.

Which crown has all three colors? Write the number and the word name.

CONGRATULATIONS!
You completed all of your
math quests! You earned:

All About My Summer

Make a timeline of your summer! Write and draw about the events in your life from June, July, and August.

Making a Timeline

JUNE

I finished 1st grade.

JUNE

JULY

Upon completion, add this sticker to your path on the map!

AUGUST

CONGRATULATIONS! You completed all of your social studies quests! You earned:

AUGUST

Fairy-Tale Friends

Write about your favorite fairy-tale character! Use an uppercase letter at the beginning of each sentence, and correct punctuation at the end of each sentence.

Elements of a Story: Describing Characters

Upon completion, add this sticker to your path on the map!

CONGRATULATIONS! You completed all of your English language arts quests! You earned:

Quest complete!

Add this achievement sticker to your path...

QUEST complete!
Welcome to 2nd grade!

...and turn to the next page for your Summer Brainiac Award!

Summer Brainiac Award!

You have completed your entire Summer Brain Quest! Congratulations! That's quite an achievement.

Write your name on the line and cut out the award certificate. Show your friends. Hang it on your wall! You're a certified Summer Brainiac!

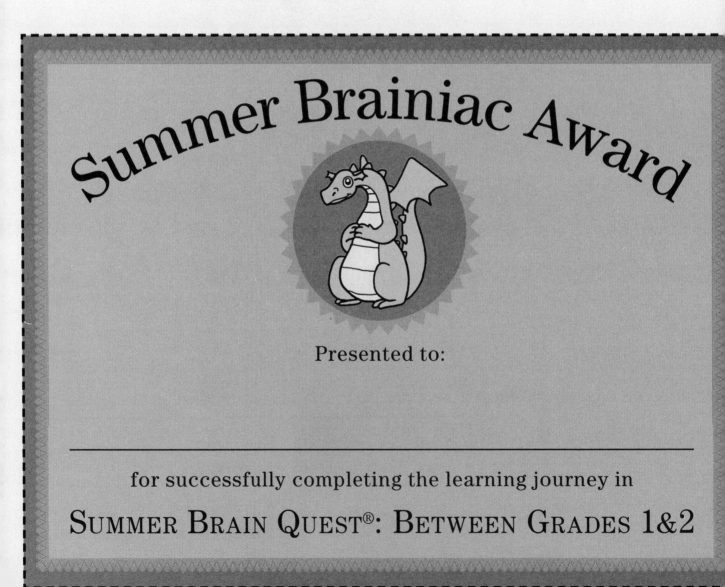

Summer Brainiac Award

Presented to:

_____

for successfully completing the learning journey in

SUMMER BRAIN QUEST®: BETWEEN GRADES 1&2

Outside Quests

This is not just a workbook—it's a treasure hunt, a number race, a way to enjoy the summer sunshine, and so much more! Summer is the perfect time to explore the great outdoors. Use the Outside Quests to make your next sunny day more fun than ever—and earn an achievement sticker.

Outside
Quests

Then add this sticker to your map!

Level 3 — Treasure Hunt

Find a partner or partners. Pick a ball or other toy to be the treasure and hide it. Then make a map of where it's hidden. Include other objects in your map to help your partner (or partners) find the treasure. Whoever finds the treasure first picks the next treasure to hide.

Level 4 — Even or Odd Race

Find a partner. Draw a circle on the sidewalk. Divide it in half and label one side "even" and the other side "odd." Drop a pebble onto the circle. If the pebble falls on the even side, choose an even number greater than 10 but less than 20. If the pebble falls on the odd side, choose an odd number greater than 10 but less than 20. Then race to gather an even or odd number of objects, such as 12 flower petals. The first person to come back to the circle and show the correct amount of objects wins.

Then add this sticker to your map!

Level 5 · Tree Texture

Trees have roots, trunks, branches, and leaves. Can you find each of these parts on a real tree? Make a rubbing of the different parts. Place paper on each part of the tree and rub a crayon on the paper to record the texture and shape.

Then add this sticker to your map!

Level 6 · Verb Race

Find a partner or partners. Select a leader, and pick a start and finish line for a race. The leader must choose a verb, such as run, crawl, waddle, jump, or hop. When the leader says go, everyone must race to the finish line by acting out the verb. Whoever reaches the finish line first is the new leader and can pick a new verb.

GO!

Then add this sticker to your map!

Outside
Quests

Then add
this sticker
to your
map!

Level 7 · Draw Your Environment

Go outside to look for natural features, like trees, and man-made features, like your house. Fold a piece of paper in half and draw the natural features you see on one side, and the man-made features you see on the other side. Which are there more of?

Level 8 · Follow the Leader

Find a partner or partners. Select one person to be the leader. Everyone else should line up and copy exactly what the leader does! The leader can bounce, reach, shake, hoot, or more. Take turns and give each person a chance to be the leader.

Then add
this sticker
to your
map!

(Level 8) Adjective Hunt

Find a partner or partners. Secretly pick an object that you see. Next, describe it with adjectives, such as "I see something white and fluffy." Describe the color, shape, size, and more. How many adjectives does it take for your partner to guess? When your partner guesses correctly, it's his or her turn to select an object.

Then add this sticker to your map!

(Level 8) Measure Your Footprint

Go to a park, the beach, or anywhere there is sand or loose soil. Outline your footprint in the sand with a stick. Find a pebble or shell and line it up with the bottom of your footprint. About how many pebbles or shells long is your footprint? Try it again with a different size pebble or shell.

Then add this sticker to your map!

Answer Key

(For pages or answers not included
in this section, answers will vary.)

Kickstart the Story!

Use a word from the box to make a compound word. Use each picture as a clue.

step	light	rain
story		bean

foot + **step** = footstep

story + book = storybook

sun + **light** = sunlight

rain + bow = rainbow

bean + stalk = beanstalk

Where Jack Lives

Circle the objects Jack needs where he lives.

Draw a picture of the clothes or objects you need where you live.

Answers will vary.

Brain Box

Even and Odd Leaves

Jack climbs only on the leaves with even numbers. Color the leaves with even numbers **green**. Color the leaves with odd numbers **orange**.

21 20 19 17 18

13 14 15 16

10 12 11

9

6 8

5 7

3

2

4

1

Jack's Beanstalk

Each part of this beanstalk plant has an important job.
Color the part that makes food **green**.
Color the part that collects water **blue**.
Color the part that carries water and nutrients ...
Color the part that makes seeds **orange**.

BONUS: Circle the objects that Jack's beanstalk needs to grow.

Jack's Plan

Complete each word with a letter or letters from the box.

c	f	p
pl	v	m

f**an**

p**an**

m**an**

c**an**

v**an**

pl**an**

Jack has a plan. Make a prediction, and write or draw what he might do next!

Answers will vary.

Apple-y Addition

Write the sum. Then draw lines to match the apples that have the same sum.

BONUS: Circle the apples that add up to 10. What other two numbers add up to 10? (Hint: There are a few possible pairs.)

4 and 6
2 and 8
5 and 5
1 and 9

3 + 7 = **10**

6 + 5 = **11**

5 + 4 = **9**

7 + 3 = **10**

5 + 6 = **11**

3 + 4 = **7**

4 + 3 = **7**

4 + 5 = **9**

Very Berry Addition

17

Draw a line to match each blackberry vine that has the same sum. (HINT: You can match the expressions without adding.)

3 + 5   7 + 4

2 + 12   5 + 3

5 + 8   8 + 5

4 + 7   12 + 2

The Tortoise and the Hare

Read the story.

Once upon a time, there was a speedy hare who bragged, "I am the fastest animal of all!" A tortoise, tired of hearing the hare boast, challenged him, "Shall we race?" The hare laughed at the tortoise.

All of the animals came to watch the race. The race began and the hare sprinted ahead! The tortoise began walking at his slow and steady pace and didn't stop. The hare thought, "I am so fast! I have time to dance and relax!" He twirled and boogied. Then he sat down to rest and fell asleep.

The hare woke up when he heard cheering. "Hooray for the tortoise!" he heard. The hare walked to the crowd of animals at the finish line. "Slow and steady wins the race," said the tortoise to the hare.

Write or draw what lesson the tortoise learned.

Answers will vary.

Write or draw what lesson the hare learned.

Answers will vary.

BONUS: Which word describes the hare? Circle the best answer.
slow   unwise   smart

Cat and Fiddles

Look at the addition problem. Then write the missing number in each related subtraction problem.

3 + 6 = 9

5 − 2 = 3

9 − 3 = 6

9 − 6 = 3

What other two numbers can be subtracted to equal 6? Write your own equation and draw a picture to illustrate it.

☐ − ☐ = 6

Answers will vary.

Cow and Moons

Draw the number of moons to show the addition problem. Then fill in the missing numbers for each related problem.

2 + 3 = 5

5 − 2 = 3

3 + 4 = 7

7 − 3 = 4

5 + 4 = 9

9 − 5 = 4

Transportation Throughout Time

People have traveled in different vehicles throughout time. Circle the pictures that show vehicles most frequently used in the past. Then underline the pictures of modern vehicles that we use today. (HINT: Some are the same vehicles that we used in the past.)

jet

rowboat

high-speed train

buggy

horse

sailboat

biplane

bike

car

Make a prediction about how we will travel in the future.

Answers will vary.

Forest Homes

Add or subtract. Write the answer.

3 + 3 = **6**

10
5
5

5 + 5 = **10**

2 + 6 = **8**

8 + 1 = **9**

9
8

2 + 8 = **10**

7 − 4 = **3**

3 + 6 = **9**

BONUS: Baba Yaga takes 10 steps through this forest. You follow 6 steps. Cross out the number of footprints you have taken. Then write the difference.

10 − 6 = **4**

29

Plants All Over the World

Read about each plant. Then draw a line to match each plant to its habitat.

A **barrel cactus** stores water in its thick stem.

Some **orchids** grow in the shade of other plants.

Moss grows close to the ground for protection from cold winds.

Kelp has deep roots to anchor it under rough water.

A **water lily's** long stem holds its leaves above the water.

Pond

Ocean

Desert

Rain Forest

Arctic

Brain Box

Apple-y Words

Complete each word with a letter or letters from the box.

m_ap

c_ap

g_ap

sn_ap

n_ap

cl_ap

m	n	g
cl	c	sn

BONUS: Complete this sentence:
The tired bird wants to n_ap.

The Golden Bird flaps his wings. Write or draw what he might fly toward.

Answers will vary.

Kitten Kin

Use the three numbers to complete the related math facts. They are a fact family!

4 + 7 = 11
7 + 4 = 11
11 − 4 = 7
11 − 7 = 4

9 + 5 = 14
5 + 9 = 14
14 − 9 = 5
14 − 5 = 9

3 + 5 = 8
5 + 3 = 8
8 − 5 = 3
8 − 3 = 5

6 + 7 = 13
7 + 6 = 13
13 − 6 = 7
13 − 7 = 6

Welcome to Candy Cloud

Follow the directions to read and complete the Candy Cloud map!

Circle the house that is located at **(2, D)**.
Write an **X** on what is located at **(8, F)**.
Draw a candy factory at **(1, C)**.
Draw an airport at **(9, C)**.
Draw a candy museum at **(7, B)**.

CANDY CLOUD

North
West — East
South

BONUS: Add a candy cane store to the map and list its location here:
(___ , ___).

Gingerbread House

Add the decorations to the gingerbread house. Add the groups to make 10. Then add more. Write the sum.

10 + 7 = 17

10 + 3 = 13

10 + 8 = 18

The Fox and the Stork

Read the story. Write each **bold** word on the correct card.

The fox got an idea to trick the stork. The fox **asked** the stork to dinner. He **made** soup in a low bowl. The stork, with his long beak, could not **take** a sip! But the fox **drank** it up.

The stork did not get **angry**. He was **calm**. Instead, the stork invited the fox to dinner. He served fish in a **tall** vase. The fox, with his short snout, could not eat dinner. But the stork used his beak and **ate** it up. The fox got **mad**. It is not nice to **play** tricks!

SHORT A WORDS

asked	drank	angry
calm	tall	mad

LONG A WORDS

made	take
ate	play

Read aloud the words in the maze. Then follow the path with **short a** words to help the stork reach his dinner.

take
ate
made
asked
say
play
tall
calm
mad

BONUS: When the stork could not eat the fox's soup, he was sad. Circle which sound "sad" makes:
short a   long a

What's Missing?

Fill in the missing number. Then use your answers and the corresponding letter to decode the riddle.

L 11 − 5 = 6
I 8 + 8 = 16
U 12 − 3 = 9
R 8 + 4 = 12
N 17 = 9 + 8
G 9 + 9 = 18
Y 14 − 5 = 9
W 15 = 6 + 9
B 16 − 10 = 6
A 10 + 5 = 15

Why was Cinderella so good at dodge ball?

Because she was always

R	U	N	N	I	N	G
4	3	17	17	8	17	18

A	W	A	Y
5	15	5	9

from the

B	A	L	L
10	5	6	6

Poetry

Read the poem and answer the questions.

A Little Mushroom House

I see a little mushroom house
with spots upon the roof.

I wonder who might live there now.
A turtle, frog, or two?

I see a tiny door and window,
made for someone small.

The closer I get, the more I must know!
Who's inside these walls?

I'll take a peek inside and look.
Oh! A teeny-tiny mouse!

She's by the fire with a book,
snug inside her mushroom house.

Which character in the poem lives inside the house?

The **mouse** lives inside the house.

What is the setting of the poem?

The poem takes place by a **mushroom house**.

Where can you look to see inside the house?

You can look in the **window**

Could an elephant live in the house? Why or why not? Write or draw your answer.

Answers will vary.

A Feather in Your Cap

Puss in Boots buys bunches of feathers for his hat. Count the number of tens. Write the number.

2 tens = 20

4 tens = 40

8 tens = 80

48

All You Can Eat

Some animals need to catch food to survive. Draw the correct amount of lines so each animal catches all of its food.

Help the squirrel eat the acorn in 3 lines.
Help the frog eat all the flies in 4 lines.
Help the bat eat all the mosquitoes in 5 lines.
Help the snake eat all the mice in 5 lines.
Help the duck eat all the worms in 6 lines.

Please note that there are multiple possible correct solutions.

Answers will vary.

BONUS: People need to eat food to survive, too! Write or draw your favorite food.

Answers will vary.

Flying Flags

Count the stars on each flag. Write the number of tens and ones. Then write the number they equal.

1 + 9 = 19
tens ones

5 + 6 = 56
tens ones

7 + 5 = 75
tens ones

Tricks and Treats

Read the story. Write each bold word on the correct card.

The Gingerbread Man

A little old woman wanted to **eat** a gingerbread cookie. So she made a gingerbread man and put him in the **oven** to bake. But the gingerbread man came alive and jumped out! **He** ran away and yelled, "Don't eat **me**!" Soon an **elk** and a **hen** chased him, too. But no one could catch him. He was **free**! He **reached** a lake, and he couldn't swim. A fox **agreed** to **help** him across if the gingerbread man climbed up his **neck** and onto his back. They swam to the middle of the lake, but the fox was playing a trick! The fox tossed him in the air and caught him in his mouth. And that was the **end** of the gingerbread man.

LONG E WORDS
eat | he
me | free
reached | agreed

SHORT E WORDS
oven
elk
hen
help
neck
end

Read aloud the words in the maze. Then follow the path with long e words to help free the gingerbread man.

oven — eat
me
he — help
neck — elk
agreed
end — free
free
reach

Here to Help

Write whether each character offers goods or a service.

Little Pig builds homes. — service
Little Bo-Peep herds sheep. — service
The shoemaker makes shoes. — goods
The baker bakes bread. — goods
Mister Geppetto takes care of Pinocchio. — service
Betty Botter makes batter and cookies. — goods

Clever as a Fox

Match the number of tens and ones to the numbers on the right.

TENS	ONES
1	8
7	6
5	7
2	9
8	6
4	2
6	1
2	2
3	4
9	5

18, 57, 86, 61, 42, 95, 34, 76, 29, 22

BONUS: The fox fooled 10 animals. Then it fooled 10 more animals. Later, it fooled 4 more animals. How many animals did the fox fool altogether?

24 animals

That Cat

Complete each word with a letter or letters from the box.

h c r
p m b

cat
pat
bat
mat
rat
hat

Write a sentence about what Puss in Boots might do next. Include two words from the cards above.

Who Lives in a Shoe?

Read the poem. Then circle the verbs.

The Old Woman Who Lived in a Shoe

I saw an old woman,
Who lived in a shoe.
She had so many children,
And loved them all, too.
So she opened the oven,
And gave them all bread.
Then she kissed them all gladly,
And sent them to bed.

Write a verb that describes what each child is doing.

Answers will vary.

read
kick
paint
cut
jump

Write the past, present, and future tense of each verb.

She ate. He eats. He will eat.
past | present | future

He slept. She sleeps. She will sleep.
past | present | future

Magic Wands

Read the spinners of tens and ones and write each number. Then compare the numbers and write if they are less than (<) or greater than (>) each other.

17 < 27

48 > 41

60 > 53

Brain Box

Spreading Fairy Dust

Tinker Bell is spreading fairy dust so some animals can fly. Help Tinker Bell find the correct animal by following directions.

Circle the animal on the hill.
Cross out the animal in front of the cliff.
Underline the animal next to the cave.

BONUS: Circle the name of the animal on the ice:
seal | polar bear

Flying Transportation

Each unicorn flies 10 more miles than each horse runs. How many miles does each unicorn fly? Write the sum.

10 + 10 = 20

20 + 10 = 30

70 + 10 = 80

50 + 10 = 60

Each unicorn flies 10 fewer miles than each dragon. How many miles does each unicorn fly? Write the difference.

80 - 10 = 70

60 - 10 = 50

40 - 10 = 30

50 - 10 = 40

Jack and Jill

Read the poem. Then draw a line to match each object to the material it is made of.

Jack and Jill went up the hill
To fetch a pail of water.
Jack fell down and broke his crown,
And Jill came tumbling after.

plastic gold cotton stone wood

Circle the correct material.

Circle the material that is **brighter**.

black shirt red jacket

Circle the material that is **softer**.

grass rocks

Circle the material that is **smoother**.

metal rope

Circle the material that is **more absorbent**.

sponge paper

66

Dreaming Children

Complete each word with a letter or letters from the box.

t e n
10

p e n

h e n

o p e n

m e n

d e n

| t | d | m |
| h | op | p |

Write a sentence about one of the children who lives in the shoe. Include two words from the beds above.

Answers
will vary.

Little Red Riding Hood

Circle the units of time you would use to measure each event.

Little Red Riding Hood was born and grew into a little girl.
years weeks

She baked a cake for her grandmother.
months hours

She picked flowers for her grandmother.
minutes years

Then she walked a few miles to her grandmother's house.
seconds hours

The Big Bad Wolf knocked on Grandmother's door.
weeks seconds

Little Red Riding Hood saw the wolf and gasped.
seconds years

BONUS: Write these words in order from the shortest amount of time to the longest: months, days, years, minutes, hours, weeks.

minutes → hours → days
Shortest

weeks → months → years
Longest

68

Tinker Bell's Wink

Read the story. Write each **bold** word on the correct card.

Tinker Bell was a **tiny** fairy with a **bright smile**.
One day she went for a speedy **zip** in the sky.
She flew **high** and did a **flip**.
She took a **dip** and a **dive**.
How her fairy dust did **shine**!
With a happy **grin**, and a **little wink**, she flew home.

SHORT I WORDS
zip
flip
dip
grin
little
wink

LONG I WORDS
tiny bright
smile high
dive shine

Follow the path with **long i** words to help Tinker Bell reach the moon.

ice bike
wit zip
grin
flip idea
dip quick
think smile
little
high ride
vine bye

Baby Bear's Bed

How many paw prints long is Baby Bear's bed?

Measure with Baby Bear's paw.
10 Baby paws long

Measure with Mama Bear's paw.
8 Mama paws long

Measure with Papa Bear's paw.
6 Papa paws long

Where in the World?

Use the compass and hints to label the continents and oceans.

CONTINENTS
Antarctica is the continent that is farthest south.
Australia is the smallest continent.
North America is the farthest west continent.
South America is south of North America.
Asia is the largest continent.
Europe is to the west of Asia.
Africa is south of Europe.

73

OCEANS
The Arctic Ocean is the ocean farthest north.
The Southern Ocean is the farthest south.
The Atlantic Ocean is between South and North America and Africa.
The Indian Ocean is south of Asia.
The Pacific Ocean is west of North America and South America.

Arctic Ocean
North America
Pacific Ocean
South America
Atlantic Ocean
Antarctica
Europe Asia
Africa
Indian Ocean
Southern Ocean
Australia

North West East South

Dragon Grin

Complete each word with a letter or letters from the box.

| sp | f | w |
| t | b | p |

w i n

f i n

p i n

sp i n

t i n

b i n

Write or draw what might make a dragon grin.

Answers
will vary.

House of Straw

Circle the best estimate for the length of each object.

15 inches
15 feet

3 inches
30 inches

60 inches
60 feet

2 feet
20 feet

BONUS: Can the width of the pig's straw house be both 10 feet long and 120 inches long? Why or why not?

Yes, because the measurement depends on the size of the unit you use. 10 feet equals 120 inches.

76

Goldilocks and the Three Bears

Read the story. Write each **bold** word on the correct card.

Goldilocks went for a walk. She saw a house and **knocked** on the door. **No** one answered, **so** she **opened** the door and went inside. She was hungry and smelled **porridge**. She saw three **bowls on** the table. She tasted the first. "This is too **hot**!" she said. She tasted the second. "This is too **cold**!" The third was just right, so she ate it all.

She was tired and wanted to sit and rest. She saw three chairs. She sat in the first. "This is too **soft**!" she said. She sat in the second. "This feels like a **rock**!" The third was just right, so she sat down. But the chair **broke** into pieces!

Goldilocks was still tired, so she went upstairs to rest. Then, then the three bears came **home**. "Someone ate my porridge," growled Papa Bear. "Someone broke my chair," growled Mama Bear. "And someone is in my bed!" yelled Baby Bear! Just then, Goldilocks **woke** up and saw the bears. She **hopped** out the window and ran all the way home!

SHORT O WORDS
knocked
porridge
on
hot
soft
rock
hopped

LONG O WORDS
no
so
opened
bowls
cold
broke
home
woke

BONUS: The bears fixed the oak chair. Circle which sound "oak" makes: short o long o

Follow the paths with **short o** words to help Goldilocks reach the window.

home toe
rose note
over
go
soft
so lost
no row
grow on

Page 78 — Spreading Seeds

78

Spreading Seeds

Read about how each animal moves seeds. Then draw a line to lead each animal through the maze to its seed and destination.

Brain Box

Birds eat fruits of plants. Birds digest the fruit and poop out the seeds while they fly to their nests.

Ants carry grass seeds and store them at their anthill so they can eat them later.

Seeds often get tangled in animal fur or feathers and then drop off the animal later. Wolves carry burrs in their fur and drop them in the woods.

BONUS: What is another animal, besides a wolf, that could carry burrs? Write the name of the animal.

Answers will vary.

Then add this sticker to your map!

79

Page 80 — Wood Houses

80

Wood Houses

These pigs have bundles of 10 sticks and single sticks to build each house. Draw the single sticks they need to add. Then write the number of sticks in all.

46 + 3 = __49__ sticks in all

25 + 3 = __28__ sticks in all

48 + 2 = __50__ sticks in all

These pigs have too many sticks. Cross out the sticks each pig should chop up for firewood. Write the number of sticks left.

37 − 4 = __33__ sticks left

29 − 8 = __21__ sticks left

63 − 3 = __60__ sticks left

BONUS: If the pig with the bow had to chop up 5 sticks instead of 3, how many sticks would be left? __58__ sticks left

Then add this sticker to your map!

81

Page 82 — Builder's Maze

82

Builder's Maze

The pigs need supplies to build their houses. Draw a line through the maze by choosing each path that has a noun.

BONUS: Write two sentences describing each pig's house. Use one noun from the maze in each sentence.

Answers will vary.

Then add this sticker to your map!

ladder · climb · protect · strong · wires · pliers · brave · electrician · wood · careful · straw · fix · hammer · bricks · nails · help · lift

Brain Box

83

Page 84 — Animals All Over the World

84

Animals All Over the World

Read about each animal. Then draw a line to match each animal to its habitat.

A **fennec fox** digs in the sand and sleeps underground to stay cool during hot days.

Some types of algae grow on **sloth** hair to help a sloth blend into trees and hide in plain sight.

A **turban snail** tucks into its shell to stay wet during low tide.

A **musk ox** grows long hollow hair to stay warm.

A **Masai giraffe** has a blue-black tongue that won't get sunburned while eating.

Rain Forest · Desert · Arctic · Grassland · Tidepool

Fishing for Stars

To catch the stars, write the sum.

47 + 20 = 67
47 + 30 = 77
47 + 40 = 87

25 + 50 = 75
25 + 60 = 85
25 + 70 = 95

34 + 20 = 54
34 + 30 = 64
34 + 40 = 74

85

Page 86 — Subtracting Stars

86

Subtracting Stars

To catch the stars, write the difference.

91 − 20 = 71
91 − 30 = 61
91 − 40 = 51

78 − 40 = 38
78 − 50 = 28
78 − 60 = 18

82 − 40 = 42
82 − 50 = 32
82 − 60 = 22

Page 88 — Feed the Dragon

88

Feed the Dragon

Color each picture that shows the dragon rider using natural resources to meet his needs, and the dragon's too!

Brain Box

A natural resource is something that comes from nature including air, water, sunlight, soil, minerals, and plants. People use natural resources to make their food, ready to build, running, and clothes.

Magic Carpet

Which of the shapes are closed? Color the carpets with closed shapes.

Draw five different closed shapes on the carpet. Then color them.

Answers will vary.

89

Page 90 — Fly Away with Mother Goose

90

Fly Away with Mother Goose

Read the story. Write each **bold** word on the correct card.

Jump on! With Mother Goose we'll fly.
On **up** to the stars **through** the **true** **blue** sky.
Hear the **music**, **hum** the cat's **tune**.
With any **luck**, we'll soon reach the moon.
We'll fly **under** the cow,
to the golden **sun**.
Flying with Mother Goose
is rhyming **fun**!

SHORT U WORDS
jump · up · hum · luck
under · sun · fun

LONG U WORDS
through · true · blue
music · tune

Follow the paths with **short u** words to help Mother Goose reach the sun.

jump · blue · hum · flute · sun · through · true · fun · cute · rule · under

BONUS: Write a sentence about a duck that uses a short u and a long u word.

Answers will vary.

91

Then add this sticker to your map!

Page 93 — Travel Through the Desert

Travel Through the Desert

Read the map key and follow the directions to draw a map.

ARABIAN DESERT

KEY
tower · city · oasis · sand dunes

North · West · East · South

Draw a city *north* of the largest oasis.
Draw another city *west* of the sand dunes.
Draw an oasis in the *northwest* corner of the map.
Draw a sand dune *east* of the new oasis.

BONUS: Write a sentence to describe where the largest tower is located. Use one of the following words: north, south, east, or west.

Answers will vary.

Then add this sticker to your map!

93

Rare Birds

These rare birds make nests divided into halves (2 equal parts). Color one-half of each nest.

These rare birds make nests divided into fourths (4 equal parts). Color one-fourth of each nest.

BONUS: The firebird has beautiful red feathers. Is the feather shaded in halves? Explain your answer.

No, because the 2 parts are not equal.

Flitting Feathers

Complete each word with a letter from the box.

f	h	k
l	p	s

s_it
k_it
l_it
_lit
h_it
p_it

A firebird has feathers that look like they are lit on fire. Write a sentence to describe the colors.

Answers will vary.

Castle Communities

Label each area as rural, suburban, or urban.

rural

suburban

urban

Brain Box

The Thirsty Dragon

Label each body of water in the space below.

| sea | river | waterfall | lake | pond |

lake

river

waterfall

pond

sea

Brain Box

BONUS: What is the closest body of water near you? Draw or write about the body of water.

Answers will vary.

Fairy-Tale Time

It's time to wake up! Draw the hands on each clock to show when each character wakes up.

Little Boy Blue wakes up at 7:00.

Robin Hood wakes up at 8:15.

Mary and her lamb wake up at 9:30.

Sleeping Beauty wakes up at 10:45.

It's time for lunch! Read the clock. Then write the time when each character has lunch.

11:45

12:30

1:30

2:15

Jot a Lot

Complete each word with a letter or letters from the box.

kn	h	d
c	t	p

h_ot
t_ot
p_ot
kn_ot
c_ot
d_ot

Write or draw what you think the knight forgot.

Answers will vary.

Helping Hand

Draw each item to help these communities.

bridge

dock

power lines

park

Brain Box

At the Fair

Which is the correct coin? Draw a line from the coin to the item you can buy with it.

5¢

10¢

25¢

1¢

Changing Forms

The wizard is organizing his lab. Draw a line to match each form of water to the correct box. Then draw other solids, liquids, and gases in the boxes.

SOLID — Answers will vary.

LIQUID — Answers will vary.

GAS — Answers will vary.

Label each form of water as a solid, liquid, or gas.

gas
(or liquid and gas)

liquid

solid
(or solid and liquid)

Brain Box

Out in the Storm

Write the name of each weather event. Use the words from the boxes.

| tornado | lightning | hail | fog |

lightning

fog

hail

tornado

Brain Box

BONUS: In a lightning storm, what should the Courageous Lion do?

Answers will vary.

Spare Parts

Help buy parts for the Tin Man. Write the amount of money each part costs.

= 31¢

= 45¢

= 19¢

= 65¢

= 67¢

= 12¢

Which part costs the most?

the heart

Tug!

Complete each word with a letter or letters from the box.

m	j	pl	b	h	r

__bug__   __hug__

__r__ug   __pl__ug

__m__ug   __j__ug

The prince gently tugs on Rapunzel's strong hair before he climbs it. Write or draw what happens when he reaches Rapunzel.

> Answers will vary.

Connect the Dots

Start at 10. Connect the dots in order to find the hidden picture. Then color it.

50   80
60 70
40
30   90
20   100
10
0   110

Fill in the missing numbers.
_10_, 20, 30, _40_, 50, 60, _70_, _80_, 90, _100_

Oranges to Orange Juice

Start the maze at the arrow. Draw a line through the pictures in the correct order to show how oranges are made into orange juice.

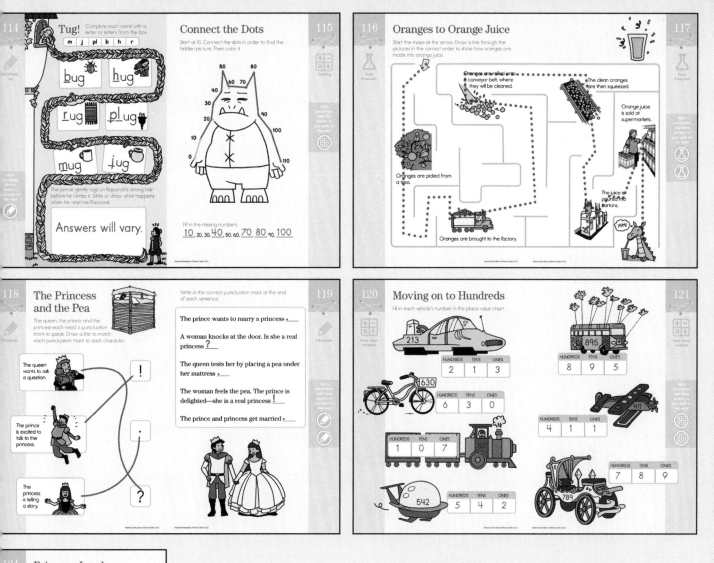

Oranges are loaded onto a conveyor belt, where they will be cleaned.

The clean oranges are then squeezed.

Orange juice is sold at supermarkets.

Oranges are picked from a tree.

The juice is poured into cartons.

Oranges are brought to the factory.

YUM!

The Princess and the Pea

The queen, the prince, and the princess each need a punctuation mark to speak. Draw a line to match each punctuation mark to each character.

The queen wants to ask a question.

The prince is excited to talk to the princess.

The princess is telling a story.

!
.
?

Write in the correct punctuation mark at the end of each sentence.

The prince wants to marry a princess _____

A woman knocks at the door. Is she a real princess _?_

The queen tests her by placing a pea under her mattress _____

The woman feels the pea. The prince is delighted—she is a real princess _!_

The prince and princess get married _____

Moving on to Hundreds

Fill in each vehicle's number in the place-value chart.

213

HUNDREDS	TENS	ONES
2	1	3

630

HUNDREDS	TENS	ONES
6	3	0

107

HUNDREDS	TENS	ONES
1	0	7

542

HUNDREDS	TENS	ONES
5	4	2

895

HUNDREDS	TENS	ONES
8	9	5

411

HUNDREDS	TENS	ONES
4	1	1

789

HUNDREDS	TENS	ONES
7	8	9

Princess Jewels

Follow the instructions to make princess crowns.

Color the jewels with a 5 in the ones place purple.
Color the jewels with a 7 in the tens place green.
Color the jewels with a 3 in the hundreds place blue.

1 7 2   7 3 5

3 7 5   3 7 7

Which crown has all three colors? Write the number and the word name.

375   three hundred seventy-five

CONGRATULATIONS!
You completed all of your math quests! You earned:

Summer Brain Quest Extras

Stay smart all summer long with these Summer Brain Quest Extras! In this section you'll find:

Summer Brain Quest Reading List

A book can take you anywhere—and summer is a great time to go on a reading adventure! Use the Summer Brain Quest Reading List to help you start the next chapter of your quest!

Summer Brain Quest Mini Deck

Cut out the cards and make your own Summer Brain Quest Mini Deck. Play by yourself or with a friend.

Summer Brain Quest Reading List

We recommend reading at least 15 to 30 minutes each day. Read to yourself or aloud. You can also read aloud with a friend or family member and discuss the book. Here are some questions to get you started:

- Was the book a nonfiction (informational) or fiction (story/narrative) text?

- Who or what was the book about?

- What was the setting of the story (where did it take place)?

- Was there a main character? Who was it? Describe the character.

- Was there a problem in the story? What was it? How was it solved?

- Were there any themes in the story?

- Were there any lessons in the story?

- Why do you think the author wrote the book?

Jump-start your reading adventure by visiting your local library or bookstore and checking out the following books. Track which ones you've read, and write your own review! Would you recommend this book to a friend? If so, which friend would you recommend this book to, and why?

Fiction

The Art Lesson, written and illustrated by Tomie dePaola

Tommy wants to be an artist, but in art class there are all these rules about what he must draw. Will Tommy get to make his own art?

DATE STARTED: _____   DATE FINISHED: _____

MY REVIEW: _____

_____

Blueberries for Sal, written and illustrated by Robert McCloskey

Sal and her mother are picking blueberries when they come across a mama bear and her cub doing the same thing. There's a mix-up on the hill—will each daughter be reunited with her own mother?

DATE STARTED: _____   DATE FINISHED: _____

MY REVIEW: _____

_____

The Day of Ahmed's Secret, by Florence P. Heide and Judith H. Gilliland, illustrated by Ted Lewin

Follow Ahmed and his donkey through the streets of Cairo, Egypt, to find out his secret!

DATE STARTED: _____   DATE FINISHED: _____

MY REVIEW: _____

_____

Fables, by Arnold Lobel

Funny, friendly, and unforgettable—this collection of fables features a cast of marvelous characters on incredible adventures.

DATE STARTED: _____   DATE FINISHED: _____

MY REVIEW: _____

_____

How My Parents Learned to Eat, by Ina R. Friedman, illustrated by Allen Say

Japanese people eat with chopsticks, while Americans eat with a knife and fork. Follow a man and a woman as they learn each other's customs.

DATE STARTED: _____   DATE FINISHED: _____

MY REVIEW: _____

_____

Mary Engelbreit's Mother Goose, written and illustrated by Mary Engelbreit

Meet your favorite characters—from Little Bo-Peep to Humpty Dumpty—in this book full of fun tales that will get you rhyming!

DATE STARTED: _____   DATE FINISHED: _____

MY REVIEW: _____

_____

Mirandy and Brother Wind, by Patricia McKissack, illustrated by Jerry Pinkney

Mirandy wants to win the cakewalk dance, but she can only do this with a fantastic dance partner. Whom will she choose?

DATE STARTED: _____ DATE FINISHED: _____

MY REVIEW: _____

_____

The Relatives Came, by Cynthia Rylant, illustrated by Stephen Gammell

Summer is ripe with possibilities! Grow strawberries, eat melons, and pluck banjos with these fun relatives during their summer stay.

DATE STARTED: _____ DATE FINISHED: _____

MY REVIEW: _____

_____

Stellaluna, written and illustrated by Janell Cannon

After an owl attack, fruit bat Stellaluna is separated from her mother and ends up with a new family . . . of birds. Read about how she adapts to bird life.

DATE STARTED: _____ DATE FINISHED: _____

MY REVIEW: _____

_____

When Sophie Gets Angry—Really, Really Angry..., written and illustrated by Molly Bang

Everything is going wrong: Sophie lost her toy, her mom doesn't seem to care, and Sophie is getting really, really angry. Will she ever feel better?

DATE STARTED: _____ DATE FINISHED: _____

MY REVIEW: _____

_____

Nonfiction

Do You Know Which Ones Will Grow? by Susan A. Shea,
illustrated by Tom Slaughter

"If a calf grows and becomes a cow, can a shovel grow and become . . .
a plow?" Answer fun questions like this one about living and nonliving
things!

DATE STARTED: _____   DATE FINISHED: _____

MY REVIEW: _____

_____

Lou Gehrig: The Luckiest Man, by David A. Adler, illustrated by
Terry Widener

Lou Gehrig played for the New York Yankees for fourteen years and
didn't miss a single game. Read about his incredible love of the sport.

DATE STARTED: _____   DATE FINISHED: _____

MY REVIEW: _____

_____

Mama Miti: Wangari Maathai and the Trees of Kenya, by Donna Jo Napoli, illustrated by Kadir Nelson

Mama Miti was an activist who encouraged the people of Kenya to grow their own trees. She taught us that anyone can change the world, one seed at a time!

DATE STARTED: _____   DATE FINISHED: _____

MY REVIEW: _____

_____

The Man Who Walked Between the Towers, written and illustrated by Mordicai Gerstein

A street performer is determined to walk a tightrope between the Twin Towers, 1,340 feet in the air, but the police don't want him to. Will the show go on?

DATE STARTED: _____   DATE FINISHED: _____

MY REVIEW: _____

_____

Sit-In: How Four Friends Stood Up by Sitting Down, by Andrea Davis Pinkney, illustrated by Brian Pinkney

When four black college students sat at a "whites only" lunch counter in the year 1960, they changed the course of history.

DATE STARTED: _____   DATE FINISHED: _____

MY REVIEW: _____

_____

Telling Time with Big Mama Cat, by Dan Harper, illustrated by Barry and Cara Moser

Big Mama is different from other cats because of one thing: She knows how to tell time! Follow her through her day, hour by hour.

DATE STARTED: _____   DATE FINISHED: _____

MY REVIEW: _____

_____

To Be Like the Sun, by Susan Marie Swanson, illustrated by Margaret Chodos-Irvine

Who knew such a tiny seed could hold so much life? Learn about a sunflower's journey from seed to beautiful bloom.

DATE STARTED: _____   DATE FINISHED: _____

MY REVIEW: _____

_____

Track That Scat!, by Lisa Morlock, illustrated by Carrie Anne Bradshaw

The best way to track animals isn't just through their paw prints—it's through their poop! Follow Finn and her dog Skeeter on their hike as they learn all about animal behavior.

DATE STARTED: _____   DATE FINISHED: _____

MY REVIEW: _____

_____

A Weed Is a Flower: The Life of George Washington Carver,
written and illustrated by Aliki

Learn about the life of George Washington Carver, an incredible
scientist and inventor who found a new way to grow plants.

DATE STARTED: _____ DATE FINISHED: _____

MY REVIEW: _____

_____

***Wilma Unlimited: How Wilma Rudolph Became the World's
Fastest Woman***, by Kathleen Krull, illustrated by David Diaz

When she had polio as a child, the doctor said Wilma would never walk
again. A decade later, she had competed in two Olympic Games. Read
about her journey to becoming the fastest woman in the world.

DATE STARTED: _____ DATE FINISHED: _____

MY REVIEW: _____

_____

And don't stop here!
There's a whole world
to discover. All you
need is a book!

Summer Brain Quest
Mini Deck

QUESTIONS

If Jack counts 5 beans and then another 8 beans, how many beans has he found in all?

Complete this sentence with an adverb: "The knight runs _____."

A magnet can attract any metal. True or false?

How long will it take to eat breakfast: minutes or weeks?

QUESTIONS

Peter Rabbit wants to pick the most blackberries. Should he pick 4 + 3 blackberries or 4 + 4 blackberries? Why?

Spell the word for the color of grass.

Bears are mammals. True or false?

Which community helper takes care of sick animals?

QUESTIONS

If 4 + 5 equals 9, what does 9 − 4 equal?

Is "sea" another word for ocean or beach?

Does dusk happen at sunrise or sunset?

How many states are in the United States of America?

QUESTIONS

What is the next number of tens? 3 tens, 4 tens, 5 tens . . .

Which word can be both a noun and a verb: duck or bird?

Which contains seeds: a pinecone or a leaf?

Which is NOT a natural resource: water, bicycle, or iron?

ANSWERS

4 + 4 is 8.
4 + 3 is 7,
8 is more than 7.

g-r-e-e-n

true

veterinarian

ANSWERS

13 beans

any adverb (for example, quickly)

false

minutes

ANSWERS

6 tens

duck

a pinecone

bicycle

ANSWERS

5

ocean

sunset

50

QUESTIONS

 If you have 8 lollipops, how many more do you need to make 10 lollipops?

 Which word can be both a noun and a verb: beetle or fly?

What flashes across the sky and is made of electricity?

How long will it take for a human to grow a foot taller: days or years?

QUESTIONS

 Tinker Bell has 4 pink wands, 6 purple wands, and 3 sparkly gold wands. How many wands does Tinker Bell have in all?

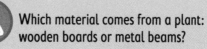 What letter don't you pronounce in the word spelled **k-n-e-e**?

Which material comes from a plant: wooden boards or metal beams?

Which community helper in your neighborhood delivers packages and letters?

QUESTIONS

If you have 3 groups of 10 golden eggs and 6 more golden eggs, how many do you have in all?

 What letter don't you pronounce in the word spelled **t-h-u-m-b**?

 Which animals have fins: dolphins, sharks, or jellyfish?

Urban areas are open spaces without many people. True or false?

QUESTIONS

Piggy drops 9 pieces of straw. If he began with 18 pieces of straw, how many does he have now?

 What word names both a flying animal and a sport item used to hit a ball?

 Which animal lives in a shell: a snail or a caterpillar?

Which of the following are man-made features: ocean, road, bridge, mountain?

ANSWERS

- 13 wands
- k
- wooden boards
- a mailman or mailwoman

ANSWERS

- 2 more lollipops
- fly
- lightning
- years

ANSWERS

- 9 pieces of straw
- bat
- a snail
- road, bridge

ANSWERS

- 36 golden eggs
- b
- dolphins and sharks
- false

QUESTIONS

The three bears build a fence around their cottage to keep visitors away. Which of the shapes is better, an open or a closed shape?

What word names both the sound a dog makes and the outer part of a tree?

Does too much rain or too little rain cause a drought?

Is a residential area mainly full of homes or stores?

QUESTIONS

What is 11 birds plus 10 more birds?

What is the plural form of the word **person**?

Which senses vibrations of sound: hearing or tasting?

What do you put on your heart when you say the Pledge of Allegiance?

QUESTIONS

A mermaid has 56 shells. Then she gives away 20 shells. How many shells does she have left?

What is the past tense of "I play with friends"?

Which of the five senses detects sour, bitter, and sweet?

What is the missing cardinal direction: north, east, south?

QUESTIONS

What shape would you have if you put 2 squares of the same size together?

In the sentence "Jack climbed the beanstalk," which words are nouns?

Is an icicle made of frozen or melted water?

Services are actions that help people. True or false?

ANSWERS

- 21 birds
- people
- hearing
- your right hand

ANSWERS

- closed
- bark
- too little rain
- homes

ANSWERS

- rectangle
- Jack and beanstalk
- frozen
- true

ANSWERS

- 36 shells
- "I played with friends."
- taste
- west

Level 1

START!

Level 2

Level 3

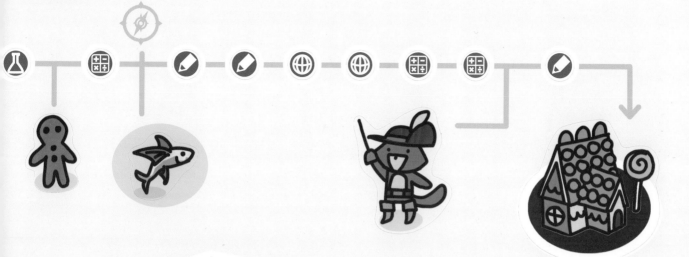

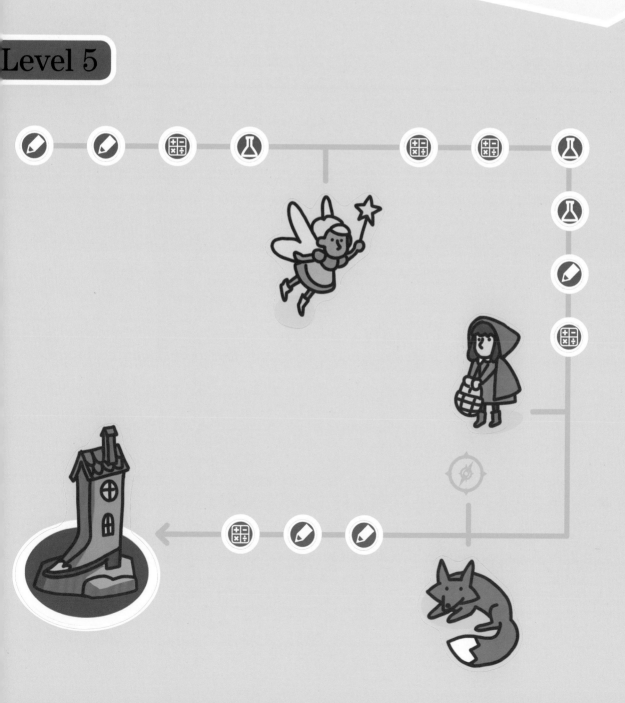

Level 6

Level 7

Level 8

QUEST complete!
Welcome to 2nd grade!

Did you sticker **every** route possible and finish **all** the Outside Quests? What an achievement!

You've earned the 100% STICKER!